Bishop Quintin Moore has [illegible] n-
tecostal upbringing in the p[illegible] e
Francis and visits to the Vat[illegible] story he tells in *Ancient Future Bishop* is remarkable; but the truly remarkable thing about Bishop Moore is how he exemplifies the hope for real unity in the Body of Christ. Ecumenism is not so much an abstract concept as it is a spirit to be embodied. What I admire most about Bishop Moore is his commitment to live as an answer to Jesus' fervent prayer that we would be one. Christians across the entire ecclesial spectrum will benefit from reading Ancient Future Bishop.

—Brian Zahnd,
Pastor of Word of Life Church in St. Joseph, Missouri; author of *Postcards From Babylon*

"From small town Kansas and a church tradition barely one hundred years old, Quintin Moore has been in Rome in the presence of His Holiness, the head of the Roman Catholic Church, and has been baptized into two thousand years of church tradition. This journey has led him to view the changing landscape of global Christianity as the Holy Spirit is bringing people together from around the globe under a fresh understanding of Jesus' love and mission. I am grateful for this testimony. It is inspiring, inviting, encouraging, and challenging. But above all, it is a journey in experiencing that Jesus said to His disciples in John 15:14, 'You are My friends!'"

—Doug Beacham,
Bishop of the International Pentecostal Holiness Church

God called shepherds, farmers, fishermen, a tax collector, a sycamore fig farmer — why not a dry-waller hailing from Severy, Kansas? Ancient Future Bishop opens up the heart of one man's journey of friendship and faith. Quintin, in raw honesty, shares his heart, his struggles, and the amazing Grace of God that has shaped his life, steered his ministry, and inspired his vision for the unity of faith in Jesus Christ. Reading this book, you will find a friend in Quintin for your own journey of faith.

— Dr. Peter Balaban

In his new book, "Ancient Future Bishop: A Memoir of Faith, Friendship, and the Dream of Unity", my dear friend, Archbishop Quintin Moore, shares with vulnerability, inspiration and deeply moving and personal insights the value and influence that friendships have played in directing and shaping his journey of faith, family and ministry. I cannot recommend this book enough. It will uncover things in you that you didn't realize were there because of the gift of friendships.

— Wayne Boosahda, Co-Founding Bishop of the Communion of Evangelical Episcopal Churches and Archbishop for the CEEC Society of St. Patrick & St. Aidan and the Diocese of St. Patrick

"With his characteristic humility and generosity, this story of faith, welcome, grief, and hope is a beautiful testimony of what unity in diversity means for us all. I loved this book."

—Sarah Bessey, author of *Miracles and Other Reasonable Things* and *Jesus Feminist*

Ancient Future Bishop

Ancient Future Bishop

A MEMOIR OF FAITH, FRIENDSHIP, AND THE DREAM OF UNITY

BISHOP
QUINTIN MOORE

Quintin Moore's books may be purchased for educational, business, or sales promotional use.

For information, please contact: Bishop Quintin Moore, QMM Press, 1505 East 20th, Hutchinson, KS, 67502, email, or info@qmmpress.com, or visit www.QMMpress.com.

Production and creative provided by Epiphany Creative Services, LLC
Cover design by Wideyedesign
Book design by Jonathan Gullery
Printed in the United States of America
Library of Congress Cataloging-in-Publication Data
Library of Congress Control Number:2019914889

FIRST EDITION

Quintin Moore - 1st ed.
TITLE: Ancient Future Bishop: A memoir of faith, friendship, and the dream of unity
p. cm.
Paperback: ISBN–13 978-1-7334599-0-7
Hardcover: ISBN—13 978-1-7334599-2-1
1. RELIGION 2. Christian Living 3. Personal Memoirs

Distributed by QMM Press
14 10 9 8 7 6 5 4 3 2 1

For Dad
Thanks for coming after me!

Contents

Acknowledgments

In no small way, this book was birthed because of a statement that my friend Terry made to me during a challenging moment in my life: "You need to trust my friendship." With that, he turned and walked back into his house. Thanks, Doc, those words changed my life.

I want to thank my brother bishops, with whom I have shared so much of this journey. Thank you for letting me walk with you. Your trust in me is humbling. To the late Tony Palmer, for daring to dream big and for being so unselfish. To Julia Elena Torres, thanks for pushing me to keep leaning into the call of God.

Len Sweet, I became an environmentalist because of you. You opened my eyes to see beyond the confines of myself and to appreciate every person's perspective. I care about so much more and so many more because of you.

Many thanks to the brilliant and tireless work of Epiphany Creative Services, including Melanie Pherson, Roy Roper, Jonathan Gullery, Gina Fromm, Alex Ferguson, and particularly Stephanie Huffman, who kept telling me I had to write this book (yes, I am excited now). Heather Ebert, my editor, I could never have completed this book without her skills and resolve to see this through. Thanks for never giving up on me.

To my staff, Lucas and Karrah Bishop, Ashley Perkins, Alexis Goertzen, Heather Hoover—never in a million years would I have been able to do this without you. Jessica Flax, you're amazing, and this is just the beginning.

Sean Faulkner, for leading our team and telling me it would all be worth it. Heather Faulkner, for letting me tell this story, or rather, insisting that I tell this story. Tanna Faulkner, without your push, this book would never have become a reality.

Thank you to Nick and Kellie, Heather and Sean, Ashley and Blain, and Stephan and Johannah for letting me tell our story without shame. Avery, Hampton, Hezekiah, Cooper, Hudson, Henley, Mancil, Jameson, Hawkston, Breslin—thanks for calling me Pops. Porter who without ever saying a word spoke volumes into my soul. You all are who and what makes me a millionaire.

To my wife, Annie, every time I went to tell a story you were there. Thank you for revealing and living unconditional love to me. I love you more today than ever. Thank you for being my best friend.

Friends, all of you—thank you. There is no book big enough to acknowledge all of you.

Foreword

"For without friends, no one would choose to live, though he had all other goods." Aristotle, the father of Western philosophy, wrote these celebrated lines to open Book VIII of his ten-volume masterpiece, *Nicomachean Ethics* (340 BC). What you now hold in your hands is a friendly book on friendship. Friendliness is not the same as friendship, so you are clinging to a two-for-one blessing.

But every blessing brings burdens and contradictions. Even your friends can sometimes be a heckling presence more than a healing salve. Ask Job. Aristotle felt Heraclitus went too far in the end, but the two agreed that opposition rather than likeness is the basis for creativity as well as for friendships. "It is what opposes that helps," and "from different tones come the fairest tunes." Aristotle also specifies in *Rhetoric* the activity entailed in the highest form of "philia" (friendship). A true friend, says Aristotle, wants for one's friend what is good, true, and beautiful, not for your own sake but for the friend's. A true friend goes beyond mere wanting and actively seeks to bless the friend with those bests.

This is a long way from a culture where friends are now a fiction of Facebook and social media. Since it launched in 2004,

Facebook has made friendship a simulacrum of images, not a tangible of touch, a list to post, not a relationship to explore. When we talk with our "friends," five thousand and under, we treat them not as unique individuals but as packets of information or pockets of interest. When you become friends of everyone, you are really friends of no one.

Opposition is true friendship.
—William Blake (1757-1827)

Quintin Moore's memoir brings us back to more ancient and biblical understandings of friendship. It reminds us that Jesus was berated for being a friend of sinners and other undesirables (Matthew 11:19). Just as David loved Jonathan despite the antagonism of Saul, or Achilles loved Patroclus above the Greek crusade, friendship will cost us something. It reminds us that Jesus called us to love our enemies; love can never exclude the possibility of friendship. It reminds us that the root word for "friend" is "freedom," and that friends give special freedoms to friends, even the freedom to take them for granted. It reminds us that friendships are rare, precious, and as cultivated as a rosebush. Bishop Moore's book beckons us to friendship as a high calling, a vocation that summons extraordinary qualities of character rooted in virtue and dedicated to the pursuit of goodness, beauty, and truth. In fact, for Jesus, friendship was the highest and noblest name for his disciples: "I no longer call you servants, but friends." (John 15:15)

One of the greatest but least known friendships is the one between Henry David Thoreau (1817-1862) and Ralph Waldo Emerson (1803-1882). Thoreau read Emerson's manifesto

Nature (1836) while an undergraduate at Harvard. Emerson's famous "American Scholar" lecture was delivered to Thoreau's graduating class, and Thoreau took it personally. The two became great friends, as Thoreau apprenticed to Emerson and worked on his farm after college while tutoring Emerson's son Edward while Ralph Waldo was away on lecture tours.

You are my friends if you do what I command you.
—Jesus

In later life, Emerson admitted that he forgot something when we wrote his tribute to Thoreau after his death from tuberculosis: "I have never recorded a fact which perhaps ought to have gone into my sketch of 'Thoreau,' that on the 01 August 1844, when I read my Discourse on Emancipation, in the Town Hall, in Concord, and the selectmen would not direct the sexton to ring the meeting-house bell, Henry went himself, and rung the bell at the appointed hour."

A friend is someone who rings your bell. Friends ring friends' bell. Bishop Quintin Moore has written a bell ringer.

—Leonard Sweet
Best-selling author of *Rings of Fire*, professor at
Drew University, Tabor College, Portland Seminary,
and Evangelical Seminary, and founder of
preachthestory.com

Introduction

> "My life is a listening; His is a speaking. My salvation is to hear and respond."
>
> —Thomas Merton

I stepped through the front door of my daughter's home one afternoon only to find my five-year-old grandson, Hampton, sitting in the middle of the living room. He sat legs crossed, holding his little chin in his hands. His eyes were closed, and amazingly, he wasn't talking.

"Hampton, what are you doing?" I whispered.

"I'm just sittin' here thinkin', Pops," he replied, his statement quite matter-of-fact.

"What are you thinking about?"

He let out a big sigh. "I don't know."

I stood silently, not knowing what to say.

"I have no idea what I'm supposed to be thinking," he continued, "but Mom told me to go to the other room and 'think about it,' so I'm just thinking."

I never questioned his mother on what she wanted him to think about, but I'm sure she had something specific in mind.

As I've reflected on the incident, I've come to realize that a lot of Christians are "just thinkin'," but they don't really know what they are thinking about. And if they do, they might not be aware of the origins of some of those thoughts.

The various facets of our society, such as culture and government, along with our faith traditions and the stories of our youth, have fit us with a pair of glasses through which we perceive the world, whether we realize it or not. Those glasses determine the way we see God, ourselves, and other people. Our perceptions, preferences, and prejudices are shaped in ways that we generally don't discern. We don't see life as it is; we see all of life as we are.

Meister Eckhart, a German theologian and mystic from the thirteenth century, wrote, "We ought not to have or let ourselves be satisfied with the God we have thought of, for when that thought slips the mind, that god slips with it."* Modern Christianity has asked us to go sit in the other room and believe in our mind and confirm with our behavior, according to a certain set of rules and rituals. Believe this, and do that, and you will know God and be okay. Rarely does anyone find the courage to question everything they think, let alone everything they've ever been taught. We just sit and stare off into space like a five-year-old, "just thinkin'."

When I was young, I was stuck in my own thinking—stuck

---

* Raymond Bernard Blakney, *Meister Eckhart: A Modern Translation* (New York: Harper & Brothers, 1941), 9.

in conflicting stories about who God is and how he relates to any of us. I needed out of this shame-based story. I needed to question everything I'd ever been taught. I was raised in a denomination that was absolutely certain their expression of faith was the right one. That certainty could have easily aborted my faith before it began—and for many of my generation, it did.

But friendships were my life preservers, lifting me above the waves of the storm. Friends have helped me grow beyond the boundaries of my childhood, my spiritual tribe, and my self-imposed limitations. Friends have challenged my individualism and my dependency on institutions. They have confronted my prejudices, shared my sufferings, and shaped my worldview. Some of these people have remained lifelong friends. Each of them has helped shape my life into what it is today, and I am so grateful to each and every one of them.

Friendship has been the primary tool that God has used to develop my faith and guide me throughout my life. Friendships are sacred because God is nothing if he is not relational; "God is only and exclusively God in relationship."* From eternity, he has existed in a relationship of loving friendship within the Godhead: Father, Son, and Holy Spirit. We have been created in his image as relational beings. Divine love searches to restore us into that relational reality of being "one" with him and with each other. This relational reality is the heartbeat of every human being. It is the key that unlocks our true identity. Without friends, we are easily lost in our old stories and a world of our own making.

---

* Eugene Peterson, *Christ Plays in Ten Thousand Places: A Conversation in Spiritual Theology* (Grand Rapids: Eerdmans, 2008), 7.

Throughout my life, every time I have faced a challenge, I have discovered a friend. The most important friendships of my life have been stepping-stones out of darkness into marvelous light. Because I was friends with a young man named Pat, I learned that my childhood beliefs weren't the only way of walking in faith. Because of a friend named Pete, I learned God actually loved me—a radical revelation to my heart and soul at the time. And because of a friend named Father O'Connor, I received the fullness of the Holy Spirit. Other friendships have led me to my life's calling, released an anointing on my ministry, opened my heart to missions, and invited me into leadership at levels I'd never have otherwise considered.

The psalmist declares, "There is a river whose streams shall make glad the city of God, the holy place of the tabernacle of the Most High." (Psalm 46:4) Through the guidance of friends, I also discovered the convergence movement, a coming together of three historical streams of Christian worship—evangelical, charismatic, and sacramental—that first emerged in the mid-1980s.

The first three centuries of the Christian church were the clearest expression of the body of Christ. But two thousand years later, after countless schisms and splits, there are tens of thousands of denominations and sects within Christianity in all its forms around the world. American Protestants have fostered division for far too long—something the convergence movement seeks to reverse. The movement's grassroots leaders, including Peter Gillquist, Bob Webber, Thomas Hayden, and Wayne Boosahda, among others, were seeking a more authentic expression of the church in the twenty-first century. They looked eagerly toward other expressions of worship. Evangelicals and

Pentecostals especially felt drawn to the liturgy and sacraments rooted in the ancient expressions of Christian faith.

In 2002, my interest in the convergence movement led me to meeting Wayne Boosahda, then-presiding bishop of the Communion of Evangelical Episcopal Churches (CEEC), an ecumenical, convergent communion of churches around the world founded in 1995. Within the next three years, I led my church into the CEEC and was consecrated a bishop myself.

Twenty-four years earlier, in 1978, Bob Webber, a professor at Wheaton College for nearly thirty years, had written a book called *Common Roots* in which he noted that Protestants had more in common with the ancient church than they were willing to admit. He argued that understanding, acknowledging, and appreciating the one, holy, catholic (universal), apostolic church of the past is essential for the ongoing health of the modern church. The body of Christ needs to maintain its continuity with the historic church.

Webber coined the phrase "ancient-future" and went on to write a collection of books in this theme, including *Ancient-Future Evangelism*, *Ancient-Future Faith*, *Ancient-Future Time*, and *Ancient-Future Worship*. Those of us in the CEEC and anyone who has been part of the convergence movement stand on his shoulders. I'm an ancient-future bishop in large part because of friends and mentors like Dr. Webber.

Several years ago, I had the honor to be in a room with one of the most well-known people in the world—Pope Francis. I was with a group of bishops from the CEEC who were just as humbled as I was by the opportunity to meet this meek and gentle man. Interestingly, he broke every preconceived idea we had about him—he turned out to be so much more than we expected. He displayed an openness and willingness to offer friendship—one based not on theological debates or institutional alignments but on deep love and appreciation for each other. Pope Francis and I are born of the same Spirit and share the same Father. We belong to the same family. Our personal journeys are very different, but the common denominator in our lives is Jesus.

At the end of our time together, we asked him if we could do anything for him. I will never forget his response: "Yes, do you know a priest?" When we said yes, he told us to ask them to coffee. "Let's take a photo together, and when you have coffee, show him the picture and tell him we're friends."

I took out my iPhone to capture a picture with Pope Francis. Copies of that photo hang in my office and in my home. Every time someone sees that photo, they all ask the same question: "How did you get to meet Pope Francis?"

My dad—my hero and friend, the man who, besides Jesus, I have tried to emulate for my entire life—was fond of saying, "If you want better answers, ask better questions." The better question is: "How did a Pentecostal country boy from Kansas become the presiding bishop of a Communion who, at its heart, longs for the unity of the body of Christ?" That's what this story is all about.

Since my first meeting with the bishop of Rome, we have repeatedly come together around a shared dream of unity among all followers of Jesus Christ, no matter our denominational background. Those of us whose hearts have been captured by God's movement in converging the historic and modern streams of Christian expression share an audacious dream of unity—not a merging of doctrines or a conformity to particular ideals but a celebration of our oneness as followers of Christ, beloved of God.

Eugene Peterson says, "Like the sacraments of water, bread, and wine, friendships take what is common about the human experience and turn it into something holy." I've spent twenty-five years promoting ecumenicalism. If we approach each other around doctrines alone, we will remain far apart. We're never going to bring institutions together. Without friendship, these conversations about our shared faith simply won't happen, but they are necessary—our disunity keeps us from being effective in reaching the world with the gospel of Christ.

We live in a culture that makes evaluations about individuals without knowing the person. We make snap judgments about situations we don't fully understand. If we would take the time to listen to another person's story, we would likely find a way to relate to one another. I wonder how many relationships have been lost due to our inability to overcome our own fear. We are afraid of our differences. We are afraid of what and who we don't understand. With the loss of every relationship, humanity becomes more and more impoverished. But Jesus has called us friends—we are all invited into friendship with God and with each other.

I'm just boy from Severy, Kansas, who was raised by Pentecostals, gave his heart to Christ in a Nazarene church, was baptized by a Lutheran, and encountered the fullness of the Spirit with a Roman Catholic priest. I started out working with my dad in the construction industry, and now I'm the pastor of The Father's House Church in Hutchinson, Kansas, and the presiding bishop of the CEEC. Every experience along this journey of discovery has been blended together for a reason—to bring me to a more authentic Christian faith and to become a passionate advocate for the unity of the body of Christ across the globe. The CEEC is driven by friendships whose motivation is to participate in answering Jesus's prayer in John 17—that they may all be one that the world may believe.

I have hope that we can recover the unity of the church one friendship at a time. The hope for humanity is in the recovery of authentic Christian spirituality. If the world could see the church loving one another, then maybe, just maybe, the world would find the courage to pursue peace with one another. Unity doesn't require uniformity but rather an acceptance of "reconciled diversity." As Christian Wiman writes, "If God is love, Christ is love for this one person, this one place, this one time-bound and time-ravaged self."*

Listen, if a boy from Kansas and a boy from Argentina can hear the music that leads to a deeper understanding of our shared identity in Christ, then so can you. Together, we have the potential to accomplish things we never thought possible. Our relationships with one another can become more important than our theological differences. Friendships based on a shared experience of God's unmerited grace are the relationships that can overcome every wall of separation. One friendship at a time, we can recover our true identity and reveal the unity and the love that Jesus prayed we would know and reveal.

---

* Christian Wiman, *My Bright Abyss: Meditation of a Modern Believer* (New York: Farrar, Straus and Giroux, 2013), 121.

CHAPTER 1

A Friend of a Friend

> "What is almost unbelievably remarkable is that God chooses friendship, available to everyone, as the means of changing the world, its people, and societies."
>
> —Michael E. Williams

"The music is the same," he said.

His voice was soft and soothing. He lowered his chin and tilted his head. As he looked over the top of his glasses, I could see his eyes fill with moisture. He glanced at his secretary and spoke quietly. "He sings the same song—the music is the same."

I was spending the afternoon with Francis, the bishop of Rome. Never had I imagined such a moment could be possible, especially for a Protestant boy from Severy, Kansas, who has been content to pastor the same church for more than thirty years. But here I was, enjoying a private audience with the pope of the Roman Catholic Church.

About a week before, I received a call informing me that Pope Francis would like for me to come and visit. I wondered if anyone ever turned down such a request—I mean, who would say no to the pope?

"Can you be here by Tuesday?" his secretary asked.

It didn't take much thought for me to clear my schedule. After preaching two services on the morning of Easter Sunday in 2017, I boarded a plane and headed to Rome—a place of mystery, majesty, and maybe a miracle or two. As I strolled through St. Peter's Square in Vatican City, the peace was palpable. Worshippers had celebrated the resurrection of Jesus Christ that weekend, and for the next three days, the Vatican would remain closed.

Dressed in a purple bishop's shirt and collar, I strolled along the cobblestones leading to Casa Santa Marta, a guesthouse for visiting clergy where Francis has lived since the conclave that elected him pope. Pope Francis chose not to live in the Apostolic Palace, the beautiful, ornate, historic residence where the pope usually lives. Instead, he prefers the more humble, common living space with many others who work at the Vatican. During a previous meeting, Francis explained that a shepherd cannot live separated from the sheep. "I'm a pastor," he said, "not a cloistered monk. I'm a people person—I live here for my own mental health."

Inside, his staff led me to an unassuming little room with six olive-green velvet chairs—three on one side and three on the other—separated by a simple coffee table. Compared to the grandeur of the Vatican, the environment seemed sedate.

His colleague, Julia, whom I've known for many years

through our work with the Catholic Fraternity, sat with me for what felt like an eternity until Francis finally entered the room, dressed in his white robes. He greeted us warmly and took a seat directly across from me. Our feet were mere inches apart.

We needed to talk about the 2017 Golden Jubilee coming up that June, the fiftieth anniversary celebration of the Catholic Charismatic Renewal, the famous Duquesne weekend, when God poured out his Holy Spirit on a group of young people from Duquesne University, a Catholic school in Pittsburgh, Pennsylvania, in February of 1967. The charismatic portion of the Catholic Church has been ecumenical from the beginning, and the Jubilee was an opportunity to further that work toward unity. I was planning to bring a number of leaders from American Protestant churches to the Jubilee.

Francis wanted to clarify how we would walk and talk together for the unity of the church. I shared with him how deeply those of us in the Communion of Evangelical Episcopal Churches (CEEC) wanted to continue working with him for unity between followers of Christ, no matter their denomination. We shared a dream of how we might facilitate more dialogue around ecumenism between Protestants and Catholics so that the prejudice between the two would begin to diminish.

"We remain deeply committed to this ecumenical calling," I said.

Francis and I are both aware, however, of the fierce opposition to this dream of unity. There are factions in the Catholic Church and among all kinds of Protestants who bristle at the mere idea of working in unity. Misunderstandings are so common, and we both wanted to avoid that. And, as in every group, some people have acted inappropriately.

With tears in my eyes, I pleaded, "I don't want this dream of unity to die. Those of us in the CEEC continue to work toward that goal. Please don't let it die. Let us continue to fulfill John 17—that the world may be one."

Francis listened intently, and when I finished, he kicked my foot with his and said the line I'll never forget: "The music is the same."

He looked over at Julia and smiled. "You bring me good people. You bring me good people." And to me, he said, "She has a very good nose."

He leaned closer, stretched out his hands, and smiled as he spoke. "I am so glad you came. I wasn't sure you could make it."

It was as if we had been childhood friends who had been unwillingly separated from each other long ago. I couldn't stop the warm, healing tears running down my face. Compassion flooded my soul.

Time stood still as the conversation continued. Personal, intimate, like two old friends, he began inquiring about family.

"How is your wife, Annie, right?" he asked.

"Yes, sir. She is well, thank you."

"And your grandchildren, you have several?"

Father Francis listened with sincere interest as I gave him a full report about my family. He wanted to know their names and their ages, as if he were somehow committing them to memory. I realized in that moment that we were simply two friends sharing our lives with one another. I had flown thousands of miles to sit with a friend. Not the leader of the Roman Catholic Church, but a humble man, a dear friend, a fellow follower of Christ. My mind raced to capture every detail of this moment, every feeling, every thought. I wanted to remember everything.

This conversation has had a profound impact on my life.

How did this happen? Why did you meet with Pope Francis? How could you possibly agree with what he represents? I have been asked those questions a thousand times. And I've often asked myself the same thing. How does a Pentecostal kid from Kansas end up becoming friends with the supreme pontiff of the Roman Catholic Church? Every time I prepare to answer, I am humbled by the fact that I had nothing to do with it. Our friendship has nothing to do with institutions nor our individual ideas. The answer is simple: I was with Francis because we shared a common friend. A friend brought us together.

The late Tony Palmer, a fellow bishop in the CEEC, and Francis had a special friendship—Tony was like a son to him. When Francis speaks of Tony, tears fill his eyes. Tony and I were also friends who had met in South Africa in the late 1990s. I was sitting with Francis simply because I was a friend of a friend.

Father Francis, as he prefers to be called, and I come from two different worlds. One of us is from Argentina and the other from America. One of us is a Roman Catholic priest and the other a Pentecostal pastor. One of us is the pope, and well, the other certainly is not. So how is the music the same? Now, let's be clear: Francis loves opera, while I like country music. But the song of our hearts resonates in perfect harmony. The Great Composer has been writing the same song in different expressions. We needed an interpreter to talk to each other, but we needed no help in communicating with one another.

This resonance wasn't happening because we were institutionally aligned. It wasn't happening because we were trying to change doctrines or merge our communities. It was happening because a deep friendship had emerged around a dream of unity in the body of Christ. The humble pastor from Argentina was reaching across the division of the Reformation, hundreds of years of conflict, and different cultures just to speak to this friend of a friend, and we discovered that the music is the same. There would be no great announcement, no historic shift in the appearance of the church. And yet in this simple room, two followers of Christ were experiencing the beauty of God through friendship.

Tony was fond of saying, “Division is diabolical, but diversity is divine.” Division hinders us from receiving and realizing the gift of who were created to be—one with God and one with each other. The things that keep us apart all crumble in an atmosphere of acceptance. The distances between us are bridged in the midst of relationship based on love and grace. Today, we need to reach beyond our differences and rediscover what is good, beautiful, and true about each other.

When we stood up to end our meeting, I asked Francis, “Will you pray for me?”

I knelt down, and he laid his hands on me and prayed a sweet prayer and blessing in English, in Spanish, in the Spirit. When he finished, I stood up. He tapped himself on the chest and bowed his head. And then I prayed for him. The least we could do was pray for each other.

That day in Rome, everything in my life came into focus. All of my experiences and relationships, which had until then seemed like a disjointed, hazy stream of unrelated accidents, revealed themselves as divinely guided stepping stones toward a deep, authentic faith in Christ and the motivating purpose for my life—to work toward unity through relationships.

Never in my wildest dreams would I have imagined, growing up on a farm in Kansas, that this would become the calling on my life.

SEASON ONE

ORIGINS

CHAPTER 2

Severy, Kansas

"Without friends, no one would choose to live, though he had all other goods."

—Aristotle

As John Denver used to sing, "Growin' up a Kansas farm boy, life was mostly havin' fun." My hometown, Severy, Kansas, has a population of about 250 people, and I was raised deep in the country. The closest store was miles from our property. The nearest skating rink was twenty-seven miles away. There were no bicycle rides to the community swimming pool. No sandlot ballpark, no neighborhood clubhouses. My childhood was wheat fields, alfalfa fields, vast blue skies, and lots of wind.

For a kid born in 1958, games weren't digital, apples were still just fruit, and television—well, there was no direct anything. Instead, a pipe wrench attached permanently to an antenna pole off of the back porch. If we wanted to change channels (there were only three), we had to move the antenna one way or another to find the signal.

My two younger siblings and I seldom went into town to play, and with only a few neighbors there were next to no opportunities to make friends. The only friend who lived anywhere close to where I was raised was Jerry, a pudgy younger kid with brown hair buzzed into a flattop typical of the era. Normal farm kids, we built hay forts and imagined defending them with our BB guns. We swam in nearby ponds and pretended we were in the Pacific Ocean. We slid down the roof of the barn, imagining we were superheroes.

Ours was a friendship of proximity, though I have fond memories of the mischief we managed to create. We didn't share a lot of the same interests, and like many childhood mates, as we grew older, we grew apart. I learned a valuable lesson from my friend, however, one that has taken me a lifetime to truly appreciate.

Like most boys left to themselves for long enough, we sometimes ended up in an argument over something. Who could jump the farthest, who was the strongest, who knows what—boys eventually have to compete with each other.

"You wanna fight?" asked Jerry.

"Yeah, I'll kick your butt," I replied.

And thus a wrestling match began. I don't think we ever hit each other. We just fell on the ground and kept from trying to get hurt, but in our minds we both beat the other one.

After a big fight, we wouldn't see each other for a few days, but then boredom ensued. One of us walked the quarter of a mile between us and sheepishly made up a story about how we had a message from our parents. This usually led to another adventure at our favorite swimming pond.

I'll never forget one evening as we were walking back to the house, Jerry bumped my shoulder and mumbled two words: "Still friends?"

And I mumbled back, "Yeah, still friends."

Though we both stood at the threshold of learning a valuable lesson about the beauty of forgiveness, in the moment, I missed it. I was too young at the time to understand. Many of us get so caught up in conflicts that we forget that all that matters is maintaining the relationship.

If I wasn't on the farm, at school, or with Jerry, I was at church. My parents came from the Pentecostal Holiness tradition, emphasis on holiness. Like the old saying goes, you don't drink, smoke, or chew or go with girls who do. But since there was no Pentecostal Holiness church in town, my parents conceded to attend a Nazarene church instead.

If I close my eyes, I can still see the flannel board figures that Mrs. Shepherd, the pastor's wife, used in the basement during Sunday School at the Nazarene church. On that flannel board, she brought to life the stories hidden within the scriptures. She told us over and over how God called Abraham "my friend" (Isaiah 41:8) and how the Lord spoke to Moses "as a man speaks with his friend." (Exodus 33:11) She explained that Jesus called his disciples "friends," even though they were deeply flawed. She told us that we too could be friends with God, not because we had earned it but because of his love for us. I was captured by those stories, though I'm not sure I knew why.

I loved the Jesus of the basement, but I was deeply troubled by the God of the main floor. In the sanctuary upstairs, Pastor Shepherd preached constantly about living holy lives—or else.

It was this "or else" part that I found so frightening. During the church service, Pastor Shepherd asked, "If you walk out of church tonight and get hit by a truck, do you know where you will spend eternity?"

When I was twelve, I walked the aisle of that little church to receive Jesus, in part because I didn't want to go to hell—a good motivator. But I also I remember the embrace of Jesus's love as I knelt on the red carpet at that wooden altar. I felt safe, accepted, and loved. The spiritual experience of salvation was real and authentic.

In the midst of all the conversation about a personal relationship with Jesus, God seemed very impersonal, to say the least. We sang "Jesus Loves Me" and whispered about the Father's judgment. Our personal relationship with Jesus appeared to rise and fall based upon our individual performance, one that was evaluated constantly.

Growing up, whether at home or in school, approval was based on performance. If you met the conditions, you were affirmed and acknowledged: "If you eat your green beans, you will be big and strong. If you are big and strong, you can go to school. If you go to school, you can get good grades. If you get good grades, you can go to college. If you go to college, you can get a good job. If you get a good job, you can make lots of money. If you make lots of money, you can get a good spouse. If you get a good spouse, you will have great kids and a great house, and you will be happy. So, if you eat your green beans, you will be happy."

The same applied at church—"if this, then that" applied to God's love as well. My subconscious understanding was that if I was clean, pure, and good, then God would really love me and take care of me. I'm sure many of us have encountered this conditional view of love and acceptance. The stories our parents, teachers, ministers, and other influencers tell us have a huge impact on how we view ourselves, others, and ultimately God himself. Many people have accepted an identity that isn't even true, but nonetheless they are held captive by it.

The God of the downstairs basement in that Nazarene church, this man called Jesus, was kind and loving, but the God of the second floor, not so much. These competing stories confused me. As far as I could tell, Jesus had come to protect us from this angry God. I came to believe that Jesus was good, but I didn't know if God was good. And if he was good, I wasn't sure he was good all the time.

The secret that no one in Mrs. Shepherd's Sunday school or Pastor Shepherd's sanctuary knew was just how complicated the Moore household was. Our struggles were frightening to me. My dad was a devout Christian and an entrepreneur running his own construction company who did everything he could to hold on to his family, protect his kids, and provide for all of us. As a child of the Great Depression, he was no stranger to hard times. His mother, Grandma Lottie, had been hobbled by polio as a child and walked with a limp her entire life. Dad had grown up watching his dad, Marion, care for and look after Lottie. When it came to his wife and children, my father followed his father's example. "A man sticks," he said.

In the 1960s, a family's dysfunction was generally hidden for fear of what others would think. In a fundamental religious context, this is even more true. You simply didn't talk about certain issues. This tension and general turmoil fueled my confusion about the nature of God. I didn't know how to trust a deity I couldn't trust to be good all the time. If I couldn't trust the constancy of God's grace, then I couldn't be honest about who I was and what I needed. Without trust, there can be no deep relationship.

It's strange how the authentic reality of God can get lost behind bad religion. But at the time, I didn't realize it was bad because I had subconsciously accepted it. The struggle in my soul about God's character was constant and confusing, and the roots of shame-based theology dug down deep. I came to believe that God was often displeased with me, ideas not spoken outright but implied. In my mind, he was never really satisfied—his displeasure lingered in the atmosphere. Jesus had died for me, but if I didn't behave, another punishment awaited. Those ideas were reinforced by those who dealt out the punishment, as if they were fulfilling God's will. They were God's ambassadors dealing out his divine justice. I assumed I deserved it!

The good intentions of decent religious people get lost in the fury of their poor understanding of God. My parents' own unprocessed trauma ended up transmitted through their claims of theological certainty. As a result, my understanding of God was neither healthy nor transforming. Seeds of distrust took root in the fertile soil of my disappointment with myself and with the idea of God. By the time I was a teenager, my suspicion was that God didn't like me much, and frankly, I didn't like him either.

At sixteen, I was stuck in my own thinking—stuck in conflicting stories about God and how he relates to any of us. I needed out of this shame-based story. I needed help. Communication in our household was nearly nonexistent, and what did exist was loud and divisive. My home life was segregated from anyone we knew. There was no escape. No exposure to any other family dynamic. The isolation was suffocating and debilitating. That's why getting my driver's license was emancipation. I now had the freedom to discover a world outside my parents' religious upbringing.

The truly saving graces of my adolescence came in the form of a few memorable friendships. Like my young friend Jerry taught me, I've come to appreciate the providence of the divine in regard to the people that come into my life. Every encounter is a blessing from God. Friendship is truly an unexpected, unmerited gift that simply waits our gratitude to unlock its potential. Another such gift was Pat, a friend from high school.

"Hey, we're going out to Lo-Mar," Pat said. "Why don't you come with us?"

This invitation caught me off guard—it was above my imagination to be included. Pat was the quarterback of the football team, the point guard of the basketball team, and the homecoming king. I was the quiet kid from the country. We truly were from two different worlds, but we soon became best friends. Neither of us could ever say how or why.

Lo-Mar was the local gathering place for teenagers. Long hair, bell bottoms, and youthful dreams—it was the 1970s, after all. Up to this moment, I didn't really know my classmates outside of school. I usually just got on a bus and returned to the farm. But the summer of 1974, right before my junior year, a portal to a whole new world opened for me. I had no idea that people could chose to be friends. I had never known you could share ideas and thoughts so freely—it was exhilarating and almost unbelievable. I found my voice through our conversations. It was a very liberating time.

My budding friendship with Pat enlarged my worldview and

opened my eyes to see from a new perspective, one that challenged my own subconscious biases. In our fundamentalist Pentecostal household, I had been raised to believe the Catholic Church was of the devil. The pope was the anti-Christ, and the whole lot of them were going to hell. (A few years ago, after returning from Rome, one of my family members asked, "What was it like to meet the anti-Christ?" Without hesitation, I said, "I discovered that he's my brother in Christ.")

But my new friend Pat was a Roman Catholic. And a good guy. I had been to his house on a Saturday night, where his entire family sat around the dining room table laughing and enjoying each other's company. His dad, Donnie, drank a beer, and his mom, Joanne, sipped a cocktail, while they told jokes and cracked each other up. A world so different from the one in which I'd been raised. And then, they all got up and went to evening Mass.

One Saturday after Pat and I had spent the afternoon goofing off and drinking beer, he announced he had to go to Mass.

"Why you gotta go to Mass?" I asked.

"Because I'm Catholic," he said, as if it were the most natural thing in the world.

That evening, I stood in the back of Sacred Heart Catholic Church in Eureka, Kansas, while Pat, his family, and plenty of other people I knew from town worshipped in the pews. The priest, a bald guy of short stature, conducted a full Latin Mass—I had no clue what he was saying until his nine-minute homily, which was extremely tame compared to the fire and brimstone preaching I was used to at the Nazarene church. At one point, the worshippers recited the Nicene Creed, stating all of the same beliefs I held.

Several different congregants went to the lectern to read scriptures—all people I knew from the community. Here were folks whose values were quite different from my family's, but I was no longer convinced they were all going to hell. I knew none of them were evil, but instead, obviously Christians.

Afterward, Pat and I went back to our escapades, drank more beer, and picked up the girls to go to a movie—and lightening didn't strike me down. The walls of my childhood belief system had begun to shake and crumble. The culture in which I had been raised left me scared to death, but my friendship with Pat opened my heart to a God who was bigger than I realized.

I had discovered there was a whole world out there different from anything I had ever known. Families lived differently! Christians didn't all share the same perspective of God that I had been given. This was liberating and confusing all at the same time. When I voiced that discovery to my family, however, my parents warned me to avoid all of them outside of our religious community. But I didn't listen. Deep down, I thought that my rebellion was really a revolution of sorts.

We have all been shaped and formed by our experiences and the set of stories we have been handed, both spoken and implied. The stories—the tradition—become the subconscious lens through which we perceive God, ourselves, and the world around us. Whatever that tradition, it inculcates itself into every facet of our lives. From this, we draw our identity and develop our worldview.

It's never wrong to rethink everything you've ever thought. Most of us have not been handed the whole story. We certainly are not all given a healthy story. I constantly meet people who imagine God is often angry or displeased with them. They see

God as a disciplinarian prone to violence and retribution. We inherited that view from people who had decent intentions, but those intentions were distorted by their own personal unprocessed trauma or religious falsehoods.

The stories that have sovereignly shaped our lives must be challenged within the safety of trusted relationships. We need a bigger story and a bigger God. I certainly did. I will forever be grateful to the friends of my youth. They taught me that we can chose to enter into conversation with each other and make a connection. They gave me the courage to look beyond my own imagination and my perceived identity.

Friendship reached beyond the dragons of my mind and touched my heart. When God wanted to challenge the limitations of religious thinking, he sent his son, who declared himself our friend. Not a book, not a doctrine, but a personal friend—one who stepped into our lives and revealed his love for us. Friendship is the basis of all true revelation of God. He chose us! He started the conversation, so the question is whether we will receive and respond to his offer of friendship.

Pat had shown me there was more than one way to live. His friendship gave me the courage to move beyond the limited mind-sets of my childhood. His friendship gave me a safe place to question the certitude I had been raised with. Our friendship also allowed me to shine a light on the trauma and confusion of my childhood so that I finally had the courage to move beyond the bondage of fear.

My friendship with Pat was the nascence of my recovery from bad religion. I had to be willing to rethink what I thought was normal. Those first steps were difficult and frightening, but a long and glorious journey had finally begun.

CHAPTER 3

Leaving Home

> "Friendships are relationships of mutual well-wishing, each person being motivated from concern for the other's good."
>
> —Paul J. Wadell

My friendship with Pat also gave me the self-confidence to pursue Annie, the girl who would later become my wife. I was this stuttering, bumbling, geeky little kid, but his friendship gave me the courage to believe. Unbeknownst to me, Annie had seen me in the eighth grade and told her friend Sarah that she was going to marry me. In 1974, when I was seventeen and a junior in high school—Annie was a year behind—she came up to me in the school hallway.

"Do you want to have lunch with me?" she asked.

Now that I think about it, I'm not sure whether it was a question or a directive. Either way, her simple suggestion was the beginning of the greatest, deepest friendship I have ever had with another human being. She chose me, and I said yes, and the next thing I know, we're at Sonic Drive-In having a hotdog. She was the best listener I'd ever met. She became the person who would listen to my struggles without trying to give advice or fix me. The discovery of an immediate friendship was a startling experience. For our first official date, I asked her to homecoming. I knew within the first week that I was going to marry that girl.

Annie, the youngest of four, came from a family who were Disciples of Christ—she was raised in the same church all her life. Her tradition—her set of stories—was staunchly different from mine. She will tell you she's never remembered not knowing Jesus. No demarcation between feeling separate and sinful and being forgiven and accepted—just always the tender, steady love of God. She was very comfortable in her faith.

My home life was fraught with tension, but Annie was going through a homegrown drama of her own. About a month after we started dating, her parents separated and eventually divorced. The challenges of our childhoods only drew us closer together—we needed each other. But the fact that Annie's parents were divorced rankled my own parents. From their fundamentalist Pentecostal perspective, dating a girl from a broken home was like dating the whore of Babylon. Today, we like to believe things have changed, but in reality, only the issues have changed. The culture we live in is still full of preconceived notions and prejudices—many of them anchored in fundamental religious nonsense.

"What are you thinking? Her parents are divorced!" Mom exclaimed.

I didn't know what to say. As hard as it is to image this now, the fact that her parents were recently divorced was outside of my parents' understanding. Divorce was paramount to buying a ticket to hell—where all the "bad" people go. I didn't care—you can't tell a seventeen-year-old boy in love that he can't see his girl.

Between our family dysfunction and fundamental foundations, I was thoroughly undone. Given the existing tensions and my willful disobedience in dating Annie, life at home only grew more unstable. In an act of youthful impetuousness, I drove to Beaufort, South Carolina, intending to join the Marines. I simply packed my bag and left. I needed something to change. I had a cousin named Dejaun who was five years older who had joined the service when he was seventeen, and it seemed to have worked out for him. I was sure that was my only way out.

More than eleven hundred miles later, I arrived in Beaufort in the middle of the night and passed out on my cousin's couch. I was finally free—or so I thought.

That night, there came a moment when I heard a voice coming from another room. I couldn't tell if I was awake or dreaming. I couldn't make out what this voice was saying, but it sounded so familiar. I thought I knew who it was, but that just couldn't be possible. I must be asleep.

I slowly opened my eyes. I was not dreaming—my dad had arrived. I was tired and sore and certainly not ready to explain myself. How in the world did he know where I was? How did he get here so fast? My mind swirled like a tornado.

I sat up not knowing what to do. This wasn't going to be an easy conversation. My feet were glued to the floor; I couldn't seem to move. All I could do was sit there with my head in my hands. The tears wouldn't stop. I could feel him come into the living room, but I couldn't look. He pulled a folding chair right up in front of me. He placed his hands on my knees. The silence was palpable. It felt like an eternity passed without a word.

"Are you going to say anything?" I whispered.

"There's nothing to say. I came after you—that says it all, doesn't it?"

My dad has always been my hero. This moment between us in South Carolina became a singular example of unconditional love.

As Henri Nouwen once said, "God is not the patriarch who stays home, doesn't move, expects his children to come to him, apologize for their aberrant behavior, beg for forgiveness, and promise to do better. To the contrary, he leaves the house, ignoring his dignity by running toward them, no need for apologies and promises of change, and brings them to the table richly prepared for them."*

The first time I heard anyone speak about the prodigal son, I didn't believe it was in the Bible—it was simply too good to be true. Now, I have copies of Rembrandt's The Return of the Prodigal Son, my favorite work of art, hanging in every one of my work areas. The beauty of the father embracing the wayward son serves as a reminder of what so many people are missing in their lives.

"Son, I will always be here for you," said Dad. "There is no place you can go that I won't find you. I love you. We will get through this together. Just trust me—I got this. Let's go home."

I'll never forget that moment nearly fifty years ago. It has

---

* Robert Jonas, ed., *Henri Nouwen: Writings* (Maryknoll: Orbis Books, 1998), 79.

taken a lifetime for what my dad did to really sink into my heart. I'm still unpacking its beauty. He planted a seed in my heart that pointed to the truth of how Jesus loves us.

Dad drove us back home slowly and with intentionality. I never doubted his understanding or love again.

We didn't solve the issues that were obvious to both of us. In fact, in some ways, everything got more complicated. Contrasted with this unconditional love for me was Dad's unconditional support for my mother. His love and grace couldn't change what was happening at home.

After months of arguing, my parents had decided I would change schools—and right before my senior year, no less. By making me transfer, my budding romance would be squashed, and my soul would be safe from eternal damnation for dating a girl whose parents were divorced. All of this was being done for my protection, out of a real love, albeit a misguided one. I remember the conversation like it was yesterday.

"Dad, I can't do that." I responded. (Surely, I was calm and collected. Or not.) There was no way I would stay away from Annie.

This time, our chairs were not facing each other. We were not looking each other in the eyes. We were driving home and staring straight out the windshield of his pickup truck.

"Well, son, as long as you're in my house, you're going to do what your mother says."

His position on the matter created absolute confusion—I knew Dad loved me, I knew he wanted the best for me, but he was also committed to my mother. But this was a different era. In Dad's mind, if I lived under his roof, I had to abide by those rules.

"I'm not changing schools," I stated.

"Then, I guess you'll have to leave."

As I glanced toward my dad, I saw tears rolling down his face. It has taken me a lifetime to understand the conflict that was happening in my dad's spirit that evening. Night had fallen by the time we pulled into the driveway. Our attempts at communication failed miserably, and all of my belongings ended up tossed outside onto the front yard. There was nothing left to do.

In August of 1975, just before my senior year, I drove to town and rented a small attic apartment—a bedroom and bathroom—for sixty-five dollars a month. Though Dad had made me move out, he privately supported my living expenses. I went to school half days and worked at a small grocery store in the afternoons to help support myself.

I graduated from Eureka High School in 1976 and went to Emporia State University. While I was in Emporia, I worked the third shift at a meat packing plant as a beef packer. Annie graduated from high school a year later, in 1977.

When we were both just eighteen, we were married on June 25, 1977, by Pastor Gilbert in First Christian Church in Eureka, Kansas. Pastor Gilbert was a good man—he'd known Annie her whole life and was well aware of our challenges. I will forever be grateful for his pastoral care and willingness to listen.

Weddings in those days weren't elaborate—at least, ours wasn't. We had about seventy-five guests, and Annie's mom made her dress and the two bridesmaids' dresses. My best friend, Pat, was my best man. Between a simple rehearsal and a cake reception, we probably spent eight hundred dollars total on the whole affair.

Marriage is a friendship that's more than "you plus me."

Rather, it's "you and me as we are when we are together."* Marriage is more than friendship, but it can never really be anything less than friendship. I have counseled so many people who were looking for many things in a mate except for the one thing they should have been looking for—a friend. I love what Tim and Kathy Keller say: "We think of a prospective spouse as primarily a lover (or a provider), and if he or she can be a friend on top of that, well, isn't that nice! We should be going the other way around. Screen first for friendship. Look for someone who understands you better than you do yourself, who makes you a better person just by being around them."†

Everyone doesn't have to be married to find wholeness, but everyone must live in deep friendship in order to be fully whole. Marriage is a way of being that deepens and broadens one's individual existence. In order to experience the true beauty of life, we must share it with another. When I'm captured by a sense of goodness and beauty, my heart reaches for a friend, but specifically, for Annie. The beauty of a sunrise or a sunset is best savored as we share it with each other.

Annie was then, and remains still, a mystery. Every page of her being stirs my curiosity and keeps me intrigued to turn the next page. Marriage is a mystery of human intimacy, a dance of trust and transparency that leads to the transformation of both people. I am so blessed that my wife is my best friend. She has filled my life with unconditional love, and she still does.

Annie says that we finished parenting one another. In

---

* Paul D. O'Callaghan, *The Feast of Friendship* (Wichita: Eighth Day Press, 2007), 22.

† Tim Keller, *The Meaning of Marriage: Facing the Complexities of Marriage with the Wisdom of God* (New York: Penguin Books, 2013), 137.

contrast to my childhood, her love has never had conditions. She knows and believes that God is good, all the time. She has always wanted God's highest and best for me. She has spent a lifetime creating an atmosphere where I can become everything that God created me to be. She does it so naturally, and she makes it so look easy. I'm not as good at it as she is. Without her unwavering goodness, my life would not be what it is today.

CHAPTER 4

Faith Renewed

> "To the Ancients, friendship seemed the happiest and most fully human of all loves."
>
> —C. S. Lewis

After our wedding, I took just two days off and promptly went back to work. My dad was a successful contractor who built large-scale projects like malls and hospitals. The month Annie and I got married, he called and said he needed help on a large project.

I had been struggling financially to support myself, and now I had a wife to provide for as well, so I was thankful for the opportunity. This was a huge job overseeing the construction of a shopping mall in Midwest City, Oklahoma. We rented an apartment in Oklahoma City where we had a glorious first year being married.

Annie and I returned to Eureka, Kansas, in the spring of

1978. My next project was helping Dad construct a new library at Emporia State University. Meanwhile, Annie went to work for Freeman Appliance Center.

We loved the small-town life. The lazy Sunday afternoons were real. In Eureka, people still waved at each other. They stood out in the yard and talked until the sun went down. Nobody locked their doors. Baseball, apple pie, and easy living. Life was quiet and peaceful.

Many of our classmates had moved on from the area, and Annie and I both knew somewhere in the back of our minds that we weren't going to stay in Mayberry USA forever. We couldn't really put it into words, but we knew we were waiting for something. To "wait" in Hebrew implies not impatience but lingering with expectation, knowing that what you are waiting on is good. That is how this season was for Annie and me. We were being held there, waiting for something else, lingering with the hope of something better. It was a healing time for both of us.

The sun was setting slowly in the west one Monday evening as I pulled into the garage. I was anxious to see Annie, and I was suddenly aware of the salty perspiration that covered my skin. The days were warmer, and the work for Dad was physical, but the pay was good. I needed a shower badly.

A voice in my head reminded me, "You need to go back to college." I shook my head; there would be time later.

As I opened the back door, the aroma of Annie's homemade fried chicken brought a smile to my face. Her first attempt to fry chicken had ended in tears, but now the dish was one of her best, and I loved it. I knew we would share a good laugh over it again. Life was good! We were both working hard, but somehow we knew that this was a special season in our lives that we needed to savor.

"Hey, how was your day?" she asked. A long kiss. "You're sweaty."

"It was long and hot," I replied. "Anything fun and exciting happen at the store?" Mondays always seemed busy for her. I headed for the laundry room. I had to get out of these dirty clothes.

"Yeah, as a matter of fact." She paused for effect. "Mr. Freeman told me to tell you that Christ Lutheran hired your cousin over the weekend to be their new pastor."

A Lutheran in my family—that would be the day hell froze over.

"Did you tell him no one in my family is Lutheran? They're all Pentecostals, you know that."

"That's what I told him," she said, turning back to the chicken. "I said it had to be some mistake, but he was convinced."

"What's his name?" I asked, headed down the hallway toward the bathroom for a shower.

"Pete something—the last name is kinda different," Annie called out. "His wife's name is Marilyn. Freeman says she's from Oklahoma City."

I stopped in my tracks. I don't really remember whether I took that shower or not.

Marilyn is my cousin on my mother's side, about four years older than I am. She had married a man named Pete who was German and a cradle Lutheran. Pete had just graduated from Lutheran School of Theology Seminary at Chicago, and Christ Lutheran in Eureka would be his first pastorate. What were the odds that my cousin and her husband would find their way to Eureka, Kansas? God truly does order the steps of our lives. I was skeptical at first, however. The dragons in my mind were on full alert. I was determined not to get caught up in some Lutheran pastor's need to find new converts.

But I liked Pete instantly. This was completely unexpected. He and I had an instant connection. He loved football, especially Oklahoma State, where he had attended college. I loved the University of Oklahoma, so the clash was on. We spent Sunday afternoons watching football and telling great stories. Our friendship found its beginning in shared interests and a shared life. I began to trust Pete enough that he could carefully shift into spiritual conversations. He wanted to share his faith, but he was patient with me. I recognize the reality of how trust and transparency facilitated a transforming experience.

"Quintin, I know you believe in Christ." He was testing the waters. "You believe Jesus is the son of God who died on a cross and rose again?"

"Sure I do," I responded.

"Then why are you living the way you're living and doing some of the things you're doing?" he asked.

At the time, I was drinking too much, among other things, and using language I shouldn't use. By this point, I was cynical and angry at what I now know was an abusive childhood, but which I didn't realize at the time. And I hadn't been to church since I was about sixteen. My friendship with Pat had revealed that the rest of the world wasn't like my family. My maternal grandmother, Grandma Jessie, whom I dearly love, was a hankie-shaking, tongue-talking Pentecostal. She kept insisting that I needed to be filled with the Holy Spirit, which, to her, meant speaking in tongues, but I never did.

Driving home from church one afternoon, Grandma Jessie

said, "Well, son, when you get clean enough, you'll get it."

Clean enough? As a rebellious teenager, I couldn't help but think, if I ain't clean enough now, I never will be. Needless to say, my attitude toward Pentecostalism wasn't very positive. The God I'd observed in Pat's Catholic Church had seemed so much kinder and gentler than the one the Pentecostals were appealing to at tent meetings, trying to cast out demons.

After we were married, I went a time or two with Annie to her church, which I thought was the most boring thing in the world. There wasn't anything there for me. I couldn't get past the questions that raged in my head about my childhood and the confusion between Jesus and the Father.

When Pete steered our conversation toward the state of my spirituality, my mind was on alert, my defenses fully awake.

"Oh, come on, Pete," I said. "I don't need your judgment. I was raised with all of those rules. I'm not going to get caught up in all of that again. Let's not do this."

I simply was not going to have this conversation, but I didn't want to lose his friendship. I enjoyed watching football with him.

"Quintin, do you know that God loves you?"

This was the defining moment of my life—this is why I do what I do today.

"What do you mean, God loves me?" I asked. "I have no idea what you're talking about."

I stared at Pete in disbelief. I had never heard that God loved me. We sang the songs, but the meaning had never registered. I remembered Mrs. Shepherd and the flannel board, but those stories had long since faded away. I wanted to know that God loved me, but it seemed so unbelievable.

Pete leaned in. "Unconditionally, it's all because of his love and grace that he accepts you. He's not angry with you. Jesus came to reveal God's love to you and for you. Jesus is God. God is like Jesus."

My heart was being changed before my mind could come to my defense. The dragons were stunned into silence. I don't think they died, but they were losing strength. Pete said a lot more that afternoon, but this statement was the most profound: Jesus loves me, and thus God loves me! Hearing his words, I knew for the first time in my life that God really did love me. I knew no matter what I did or how I stuttered or stumbled, God loved me—without conditions or restraints. Not because I performed, but because I was his child.

Pete had ripped off the burial garments of religion. He pulled the rug out from under the need to perform. In C. S. Lewis's novel, *The Voyage of the Dawn Treader*, he describes a troubled boy named Eustace whose hardened heart morphs him into a dragon. There is nothing Eustace can do to change himself. Instead, the lion Aslan has to shred his scaly skin to release him and reveal his tender interior.

"And there was I as smooth and soft as a peeled switch and smaller than I had been. Then he caught hold of me—I didn't like that much for I was very tender underneath now that I'd no skin on—and threw me into the water . . . I'd turned into a boy again."*

Pete had ripped the skin off of the dragon. I now stood beside Eustace. That afternoon, hanging out and watching a football

* C. S. Lewis, *The Voyage of the Dawn Treader* (London: Puffin Books, 1979), 96.

game on TV, turned out to be the most earth-shattering moment I'd ever experienced. That moment will forever be imprinted on my soul. Loved! Simply loved for being me. I was a boy again, renewed. I didn't know it, but I'd begun discovering my true identity as a child of God.

A week after our conversation over football, Pete enrolled me in a ninth-grade catechism class—literally. Seven high school freshmen, plus me, two years out of high school. There I was in a basement again. In the basement of Severy Nazarene, Mrs. Shepherd had recounted the Bible stories about Abraham, Moses, David, Gideon, Peter, and Paul, all in living flannel. In the basement of Christ Lutheran, I was exposed to grace through faith. The next few months were filled with the joy of discovery. I learned that faith is received, not achieved. I realized that we are who we are because of grace alone. "The faith which was once for all delivered to the saints," we don't get to make it up—it is given to us "as is."

We studied from *Word and Witness: Understanding the Bible* by Foster Roland McCurley Jr. We learned about the Lord's Prayer, the creeds, water baptism, and the Eucharist. I was completely unprepared for the liturgy of the Lutheran church. The prayer book, the order, the history of it all, who knew? In place of the certainty of my childhood religion, I was being exposed to something other—known and yet unknown. I was caught in the mystery of it all.

On Sunday mornings, in lieu of heavy scriptural dissertations from the pulpit, Pete told stories. I didn't realize it at the time, but hidden in the stories were truths, glimpses of a God I had never really seen. My heart was hearing something for the first time.

The most powerful streams are never straight. The best rivers find their way through the mountains and fields of life. The strongest rivers are made up of many streams that converge into one great river. A Nazarene stream met a Lutheran stream in the midst of a Disciples of Christ stream with a Pentecostal tributary to boot. I could feel the river moving in my soul deeper and deeper.

After the catechism classes were complete, I was confirmed at Christ Lutheran Church. That Sunday, I knelt at the altar where Pete baptized me with a handful of holy water. As I waited for the Eucharist, my head still damp, my heart pounded, and tears streamed down my face.

"The body of Christ broken for you," Pete said, pressing a wafer into my palm.

I could feel the Lord's presence! Real presence, a spiritual experience, just like I had felt at that altar in the Nazarene church when I was twelve. Just like when Grandma Jessie prayed in tongues, I knew the Lord was filling my heart, but more than that, he was present to everyone in that sanctuary.

I still have people ask me what happens to the bread during Eucharist. I still don't know if I would argue any position on the matter, but what I know is that we were told to "do this in remembrance." In the obedience, something happens. Christ is present at his table.

Deeply touched, I returned to my place in the pew. When I sat down and looked around, my jaw dropped. Every Lutheran in the place was stone-faced. They weren't experiencing anything in a visible way.

On our way out, I asked Pete, "What's wrong with these people? Don't they know that was the real presence of God?"

"Oh, Quintin—that's just your Pentecostalism showing forth," he said.

No, it wasn't. I was ashamed of my Pentecostalism. I had ventured way out of Pentecostal Holiness territory—my grandparents would have preferred I stay drinking at the bar than attend a Lutheran church. This wasn't that. But Pete didn't know how to explain it either.

My experience in the Lutheran church lit a fire in my heart to become a Lutheran minister. I kept working for my dad and trying to keep up with my classes at Wichita State, where I'd finally enrolled, all the while begging my dad to let me go to seminary. I wanted to be a pastor, but my dad didn't think that was a good idea.

"Son, you'll starve to death," he said. "Preachers don't make any money. Just stay put."

Dad dreamed of the whole family working together in the business he'd built. Annie and I had moved with our eldest son, Nicholas, who was born in August of 1980, from Eureka to Wichita, where Dad's business was headquartered. For the next four years, I worked for Dad building hotels, apartment complexes, and other commercial businesses.

I managed to steal away and take Bible classes on Tuesday and Thursday nights. One of my classes was "Life of Christ" taught by an Irish Catholic priest named Father O'Connor, a handsome man well over six feet tall. He had been a priest for more than forty years, and he had a gentle, kind spirit.

After class one evening, he invited me to a campus Bible study.

"Don't you have Pentecostal in your background?" asked Father O'Connor.

"Yes, I do," I admitted, more than a little mortified that he knew that.

"Well, there's a guy doing a Bible study in the basement of the library. Would you go with me?"

"Sure, I'll go," I said, though I didn't really want to go.

Unbeknownst to me, the young Bible study teacher was a leftover of the charismatic Jesus movement, a former Assembly of God minister who was now nondenominational. Full of joy, he made the stories of Jesus come to life as if I were right there next to the disciples.

"Every good and perfect gift is from above, coming down from the Father of the heavenly lights," said the teacher. "If you see anything in me that is good, it is from the Father above. He wants to give you everything good. Come here, and I will pray for you, and you will know of his goodness."

Father O'Connor nudged me. "I want that, don't you? I want that goodness. Look at him—I want his joy!"

We moved to the front where the young teacher laid hands on us and prayed. The next thing I knew, Father O'Connor was laughing and jumping up and down. Well, this is a little unusual. He couldn't stop laughing. He was very proper—this was out of character for him.

Only a moment later, I started having the same experience. Laughing, jumping, overwhelmed with the reality of joy—joy that wasn't emulating from something outside myself but from inside with no apparent reason or cause. And peace! A river of peace flooded my soul. Glorious joy and peace—I knew the Lord himself was present, and not simply in an emotional way. I was being infused with his very life.

That day, my friend Father O'Conner and I experienced what

Douglas Moo calls an "abundant extravagant effusion" of God.*

Though I didn't understand this experience theologically, I knew it was directly connected to the One who met me at that little altar back in Severy. The knowledge of his love that Pete had shared with me was the love I was now feeling somewhere deep within. I was truly tasting the goodness of God, and I would never again be satisfied with less. For the second time, I was vividly aware that I was accepted—I belonged.

Many corners of Christianity claim the charismatic experience is simply emotional, but I'm in good company. Paul exhorted believers to sing and make melody in their hearts to the Lord (Ephesians 5:19), and the disciples were filled with the joy and with the Holy Spirit (Acts 13:52). From that moment in the campus Bible study, my desire has been to be continually filled.

It took me weeks to get my head around the fact that my experience of the Holy Spirit in that campus Bible study is what my grandparents had been talking about. The Pentecostal expression I'd been raised with looked different—old ladies ran the aisles with hankies, screaming and shaking, a wild blend of charismatic and Native American spirituality. These women never cut their hair or wore makeup or pants. The teacher from the Jesus movement was happy and more toned down and not nearly as legalistic.

The leader of the Bible study told me over and over again, "Unless you get a telegram telling you God has changed his mind, then what he said in the scriptures is truth for us today."

---

* Douglas Moo, *The Epistle to the Romans: The New International Commentary on the New Testament* (Grand Rapids: Eerdmans, 1996), 304.

I began to expect God to do things in my daily life. I prayed for anything and anyone, which is exactly what Jesus did. In one of my classes, a robust woman named Rosie sat next to me.

"Quintin, I cannot get my breath," she said.

"What's the matter?" I asked, concerned.

"I'm having a bad asthma attack," she said.

I could tell she was struggling to breathe. I leaned across the aisle and whispered, "I don't know if this makes any sense, but I'm going to this Bible study, and the guy there says that if you lay hands on one another in Jesus's name, it helps." I secretly hoped she would want nothing to do with my suggestion.

"I guess it can't hurt," she said between gasps for air.

I leaned closer and spoke a timid prayer. "Jesus, the guy from the Bible study says I can do this, so I'm doing it . . . oh yeah, in Jesus's name."

We finished praying just as the professor walked in to begin his lecture. Rosie and I turned around and started listening. He droned on for about twenty minutes when Rosie suddenly stood up.

"Hey, I can breathe!" she declared. "Who did you say that guy is? Where do I find him? I want to ask him some questions."

Needless to say, the professor was not at all impressed with my explanation for the outburst.

The Holy Spirit works to continually magnify our sonship and clarify our identity as children of God. The Holy Spirit also increases our capacity to communicate with God. The Lord had reached past the religious paradigms of my youth and touched my heart. The dragons of my mind were left whimpering in the dust.

At this point, however, the Lutheran Campus Ministry

wanted nothing to do with me because I was praying for my classmates to be healed, speaking in tongues, and singing to new worship music. None of this was kosher for the Lutherans in the early 1980s. My colleagues reminded me that Lutherans didn't believe in speaking in tongues or laying hands on people to ask God for healing. I sat with my advisor and several other gentlemen, weeping.

"I want to be a Lutheran minister more than anything," I said. "But you need to explain Acts two to me."

My advisor closed my Bible. "I can't explain it to you, but we don't believe in those things."

The convergence of these experiences was clear. God reveals himself in myriad ways. Every stream of the church wants to say they have the "right" way, but the reality is that we need each other. We need to encounter God in scripture, sacrament, and spirit. I didn't understand everything at that moment, but today I am grateful for every expression of God's grace in my life.

I started reading C. S. Lewis and J. R. R. Tolkien and at the same time listening to every charismatic preacher I could find. I couldn't get enough of Orthodox theology, but I was in love with the gifts of the Holy Spirit. Father O'Connor had given me a copy of the Anglican prayer book, the Book of Common Prayer, and yet he and I would join hands and pray in the Spirit.

I was living in this collision of charismatic and contemplative spirituality, and I was loving it, but I realized I no longer fit in anywhere. Where did this leave me? I needed a mentor. I needed a community of people who would let this confluence of expression develop.

In this moment of crisis, Annie and I felt lost in choosing

the right church. How were we supposed to pick and choose between these streams we had discovered? I called my grandmother for advice.

"Quintin, I've been praying for you," Grandma Jessie said. My grandmother was always praying. She believed prayer was the answer to everyone's problems. "Do you remember Brother Crane? He's living right near you. I think you should go talk to him." And with that, she hung up.

Reverend Lloyd Crane had been my grandparents' pastor for years—a Pentecostal preacher through and through. Lloyd was in his eighties and happily retired. In my wildest imagination, I couldn't see what we could share of value. But Grandma Jessie wouldn't leave it alone, so I finally went to see him.

I sat out in the truck for a long time before I walked up those old wooden steps to Lloyd's trailer house, still unsure. The door flew open before I could turn back.

"I wondered how long you were going to sit out there," said Lloyd. "Come on in, son. I've been expecting you."

Lloyd and I were instant friends. I hadn't anticipated it, but it was profound. Just like Pat, Pete, and the priest, I needed another friend.

He retreated back to his chair. "Don't you know that confusion is not of God?" Once he started, he didn't slow down. "God is leading you into a wide place. You need to relax and enjoy the journey. There is so much more to God than anyone has ever imagined. Don't let anyone—including me—put you into some old religious box. Now, do you like baseball?"

This old pastor didn't look down on my Lutheran experience or insist that Pentecostals had it all. He encouraged me that God had a purpose for my life and that he was working through every part of the church to bring about his divine plan. God was bringing me into a better understanding of who he is and who I am.

Of all places, Annie and I ended up in a small Pentecostal Holiness church in Derby, a suburb of Wichita, where Reverend Lloyd Crane had last served. We never received communion or witnessed baptisms in this church, but they loved us, and we loved them. I taught Sunday School and led youth camps. I loved the pastor, and he was very kind to me. He allowed me to preach for him from time to time, and I filled in at other churches in the area.

All the while, I kept working for Dad and taking classes, and Annie and I kept waiting for something we couldn't even name.

CHAPTER 5

The End Is My Beginning

"In my end is my beginning."

—T. S. Eliot, "East Coker," Four Quartets

My family and I stood dazed and frozen. As snow swirled around the casket, the tent played a mournful tune. Metal hooks kept beating against the aluminum poles that swayed in the wind. I will never forget that sound. The notes of that song became one of the soundtracks in my soul.

The wind blew right through the layers of our clothing as the preacher droned on and on. Someone should have told him that nothing he said could have warmed our hearts or our bodies that day.

The previous four days had been simply unthinkable. On December 16, 1985, my dad died of a massive heart attack. He was forty-nine years old. Christmas was only five days away, but there was no joy in our hearts. No thoughts of celebration, only fear of the unknown and unacknowledged anger.

I stared into the faces of my wife and children and realized that we were in the midst of a process over which we had no control. This moment would change everything. My faith was dashed—destroyed. It felt disingenuous to reassure my loved ones that everything would be okay when I knew full well that it would never be okay. My grief consumed me. The only way I could overcome it was to look straight at it. I had to give myself permission to suffer in order to continue living. I would have to come to a new understanding of faith in the midst of the pain.

Sometimes we don't fully appreciate someone until they are no longer around. The older I got, the smarter my dad seemed. He was my biggest fan, though I often didn't know it. My friendship with Dad was forged through many challenges that had at times clouded my vision. The last few years of his life, we became extremely close, and I truly wish there had been more time. My dad was a true friend who always wanted my best.

The reality of who we are is often buried so deeply that only through suffering can we uncover that authentic self, which is in fact our own soul. A self can be developed by all kinds of gurus and gimmicks, but souls are only discovered and developed by sharing our lives with others and experiencing the suffering of love and loss.

Dad's death uncovered my soul.

I stood there in the cold Kansas wind, staring at a deep hole in the ground. All hope appeared gone. Our faith has never forbidden our human feelings, but we must never allow our feelings to destroy our future. Our hope is never found in the graves of the past but in the hope of God's ultimate plan for our lives. When we walk in these wilderness moments, we must resist the temptation to look back toward Egypt. Faith knows the sun rises every morning, and God's mercies are new every day.

My dad's passing was the most significant turning point of my life. An epic shift. Ground zero. From there, everything had to be rebuilt. Memorials not only mark the end of something, but also the beginning of a new normal, yet to be defined. It's been more than three decades since I stood beside my father's grave on the cold Kansas prairie. I had no perception that God was setting the stage for his plans and purposes to come to pass. At that moment I didn't understand the ways of God's movement.

As shock gave way to grief and then to anger, I continued to cry out to God for understanding and direction. In the darkness, brief moments of clarity, like lightning flashes during a Kansas storm. We took a few steps down a certain path until the way closed. And then another was revealed. For the second time in our lives, Annie and I found ourselves in this holding pattern, only now we were a family of five. Making decisions that will affect three young kids seemed only more difficult. We needed direction, a sense of calling.

In the weeks and months that followed my dad's death, the comfort of the Lord came to me in the form of a dream. The pictures were so clear. They weren't new images, but old ones imprinted on my heart. Everyone in Kansas who knows anything knows something about wheat. The image of golden wheat is embedded in our psyche.

When the cool fall breeze blew across the fields, farmers sowed their seeds in the dark Kansas soil. I remember watching the snow-covered prairie give way to a beautiful green carpet as stalks burst through the rich dark ground. The cold winds of winter turned into constant blasts of hot air that caused the golden heads of fruit to sway against each other. Like a lullaby, the sound of wind-blown wheat lulled me to sleep many hot Kansas nights. Even now, I can almost feel that summer air against my face; the rhythmic sound still soothes my soul.

During those blistering June days, I watched as everything else ceased. No one painted barns or worked on equipment. Only one focus—the harvest. Every effort, every ounce of energy, went into bringing in the crop before something damaged the fruit.

The dream was the same, night after night—this golden wheat from my childhood. One night, I woke up startled, as if someone had shaken me awake to tell me something. I wasn't awake but alert, ready. What was it that I didn't understand? And then a voice so familiar to my spirit said, "Most assuredly, I say to you, unless a grain of wheat falls into the ground and dies, it remains alone; but if it dies, it produces much grain."

A seed contains within it the potential of a vast harvest. A seed is the source, the origin, the beginning. In every seed is the promise of something larger than itself. The harvest is in the seed. The miracle is in the seed. The tough part is that it must die in order to release that potential.

Every good farmer knows this. They plant seeds into the ground every fall, in faith. Those farmers of my youth never fretted when the snow came and the ground froze. They understood what was happening to that seed. "Foolish one, what you sow is not made alive unless it dies." (1 Corinthians 15:36) "But if it dies, it produces much grain." (John 12:24)

The only way to get the full benefit of that seed was to allow it to go through the process of dying. There alone in the darkness of that planted place, the exterior covering of that seed breaks down under the chemical reaction of the soil. I doubt that it's even necessary for a farmer to understand the chemical process in order for it to work. They just simply trust that it does, and they benefit from the process that God established long before they ever thought about their crop.

Everything we see in the natural world is a reflection of the spiritual kingdom of God. If we can grasp these principles, we can begin to understand the nature of God's kingdom. "I know what I'm doing. I have it all planned out—plans to take care of you, not abandon you, plans to give you the future you hope for." (Jeremiah 29:11, MSG)

In early 1986 after Dad had died, I was about to leave work late one evening. I wanted to go home because I wasn't accomplishing anything anyway. The business wasn't going to make it, and my family was fractured. My mother and I were estranged, which blocked me from properly taking over Dad's business, as he had desired. His dreams had become my dreams, and now it was clear that shared dream was dead, too.

The last of our crew had left the office around 6:30 p.m., but an hour later, I was still lingering in my office. I needed to finish an estimate on a new project—the plans were spread across my planning table, which faced a wall hung with various blueprints. All of a sudden, I felt some kind of presence behind me. When I turned around, I thought Dad was in the room sitting in one of the chairs opposite my desk.

As I moved around the desk, I found myself overcome by divine light. Overwhelmed, I found myself on the floor, weeping, sobbing tears upon tears. I needed answers. I cried out, "What am I to do with this business? What am I to do with these employees?"

Tenderly came a whisper. "You have a business and employees—I'll take them."

My sobs deepened. "What about the buildings, the materials, the projects?"

Without hesitation, the whisper said again, "I'll take them."

Time seemed to stop. "What about my mom, my sister, my brother?"

The voice was stronger. "They are mine as well."

First Dad and now this—I couldn't comprehend what was happening. God was removing everything in my life that felt real to me. The crying turned into whimpering, my breathing shallow. "What about Annie and the children?"

The tenderness was back. "They too are mine."

I'm not sure I moved. I can still feel the tears that made rivers down my face.

"Me, what about me?"

Silence. And then: "You, son, that's want I want. I want you!"

The conversation was over, the direction determined. I had no idea what the future held, but at least I knew there was one. Sometimes it's enough to know there is a future.

I had known for several years that the Holy Spirit was leading me into something beyond, but I couldn't quite grasp what it would look like. Dad and I had talked many times about what I was feeling. He had shared his concerns and encouraged me to wait, saying the time wasn't right. I certainly hadn't anticipated the series of events that emerged.

Annie and I slowly leaned into the future, as uncertain as it seemed. In the end, we sold off everything. As I worked to close my father's business, Annie made plans to sell our home. We knew that the Lord was leading us somewhere else, though we had no idea where. "Leave your land, your relatives, and your father's home. Go to the land that I will show you." (Genesis 12:1, GW) The words sound romantic until you have to obey them.

Every time I read about Abraham, I'm reminded of what the apostle James said: "Abraham believed God . . . And he was called the friend of God." (James 2:23) Abraham spent his life following God around in the wilderness. Like Abraham and Sarah, we left our home and headed out into a land for which we had no map, but we knew it was "the land of the living." We had come to that place in our lives that we trusted in God's love for us. We didn't know what the future held, but we knew were not alone.

I knew God had plans for me, but I couldn't have guessed where he would lead. During prayer, I heard words spoken from somewhere deep in my soul: "refugees of darkness." But who were these refugees and what was I supposed to do with them?

In October of 1986, the district superintendent of the Pentecostal Holiness denomination called. He had heard that I planned to pursue a degree in theology from Bethany College, a Lutheran school in Lindsborg, Kansas. He asked me if I would consider preaching at a little church in Hutchinson, a town of barely forty thousand people about forty miles from Lindsborg. There were about fifteen Pentecostal Holiness churches in Kansas at the time, and this church was dying—the congregation consisted of twenty-two people.

That first Sunday at the Abundant Life Church in Hutchinson, I was only there to fill the pulpit. A test run. But as Annie and I sat down with our three little children, we were both stunned by the nudge of the Holy Spirit. (We've come to believe that generally the Spirit nudges and hugs us into his purpose.)

She elbowed me. "We're moving here, aren't we?"

"Yeah, I believe we are."

Our eyes met, and simultaneously we both knew we were moving to this community. We didn't know why, but we knew we were.

The subject of my sermon was "What do the righteous do when the foundations have been shaken?" I'm convinced I was basically preaching to myself, even though twenty-two other people sat there listening. Annie and I drove home from Hutchinson in silence. We knew we could trust our Friend, but could we trust ourselves?

One evening outside our church in Derby, my friend Mark and I stood next to my pickup truck. He and I had become close friends over the last few years. We both served together as deacons, and Mark and his wife, Roxie, were one of the young couples who attended a Bible study I taught on Friday nights. They knew we longed for the Eucharist of the Lutheran church, a different kind of teaching than the Pentecostals were giving, but they didn't judge us. Mark and I loved our little community church and worked hard for its health. We shared lots of the same challenges of being young and married. We talked easily and often.

"I don't know whether I can do this," I said. "I don't know if I can pastor. I've never thought of this in my life—not really, not like this."

Mark stood there for several hours and listened as I mulled over my apprehensions and fears. He simply listened to me wrestle with God. I finally ran out of words, and we stood there together, in silence.

Mark chose his response slowly and intentionally. "Quintin, you're not going to be a pastor—you already are one. You're the best pastor I have ever known."

At those Friday night gatherings, Annie cooked a meal, and I shared a message from the scriptures. I didn't realize I was pastoring—I was just loving people. Mark's words were life to me. Simple, concise, and yet breath to a dying man. What I didn't understand was that pastoring wasn't something I do but rather something I was created to be and am still becoming. Mark's kindness to patiently listen to my fears and quietly nudge me to see beyond them forever changed my life.

I called Lloyd to tell him God had spoken to us.

"Keep your mouth shut," he responded. "If it's God, it'll work out. If it isn't, it won't."

That first Sunday in October of 1986, we put our house on the market. Several weeks later, on November 9, the district superintendent called again and told us that the congregation in Hutchinson—all twenty-two of them—had voted for me to be their pastor. I'm still overwhelmed. It remains the most humbling reality of my life.

Our house sold the same day.

"After you've baptized their children and buried their parents," said Lloyd, as he gave me his blessing, "after you've married their children and looked at the pictures of their grandchildren, then you will be their pastor. For now, it's just a dream."

Somewhere between Mark's encouragement and Lloyd's prophecy, I found the footing to move forward into the future. And thank God, we're still moving!

SEASON TWO

THE CHURCH

CHAPTER 6

Abundant Life

"We walk among worlds unrealized, until we have learned the secret of love."

—Hugh Black

When I was a child visiting my grandparents in Oklahoma, I got lost, or so Grandma Jessie told me. I don't remember being lost or feeling lost. I remember the smell of the fertile red soil. It felt cool standing in shade, gazing at sunbeams that flickered through corn stocks twice as tall as I was. I felt safe, serene, at peace.

I wasn't afraid—quite the opposite. I felt surrounded by something unseen and yet familiar, something peaceful and secure. I often chose to return to that place in my mind—I still do, to this day. The same thing always happened—I didn't understand my grandparents' reaction when they found me and pulled me into their embrace. They were so happy to have found me.

Years later, when Grandma explained what happened, I began to cherish the memories even more.

Annie says I was lost those first months of being in Hutchinson. She often found me in the sanctuary of the church next to our parsonage. Again, I don't remember feeling lost—I felt free.

"Quintin, take my hand," she said. "Let me help you back to the house."

She led me across the yard to the little house that sat next door to the church.

"What time is it?" I asked.

"Oh, it's about five," she replied.

Maybe I was lost again and didn't know it. Again, I was surrounded by something warm and safe. I remember knowing that I was close to someone in a way that I had never known.

Every morning during those first months in Hutchinson, I walked across the yard from the parsonage to the church, intending to spend an hour in prayer before going to work as an estimator for local contractors. But I never made it out of the sanctuary. Every day for the next several months, I kept getting gloriously lost. I literally was captured by God's presence.

Prayer is a way of life, a mode of being that takes us beyond time and space to a place beyond our imagination.

"To pray, then, is more about listening than about talking. To pray is to be centered in love; it is to let what is deepest within us come to the surface. For me, it is all that and more. Prayer is also a meeting with the One who loves me, who reveals to me my secret value, who empowers me to give life, who loves us all, and who calls us forth to greater love and compassion.

Prayer is resting in the quiet, gentle presence of God."*

According to Celtic tradition, this thin, sacred place is where the veil that separates heaven and earth is nearly transparent, a place where one can experience a deeper sense of God's presence. For a moment, the spiritual and natural worlds converge. From here, you can see into eternity. The divine breaks through the veil of substance and penetrates the soul. Here, the reality of communion with him is tangible and known—not an intellectual knowing but something higher and deeper. This profound, unexplainable experience can be a sudden, momentary awareness of his presence or a sustained reality.

Prayer is like breathing—it sustains real life. God breathed into Adam, and he became a living soul. I was breathing differently. Every breath filled with grace and every utterance filled with praise. The more I prayed, the more I knew God loved me, not because of what I did or didn't do, but because he is love. "We walk among worlds unrealized, until we have learned the secret of love."†

Experiencing unconditional love in a conditional world is exhilarating. I didn't—and still don't—want to do anything other than live in this constant conversation with the Lord. I talk; he listens. He talks; I listen. Simple, really—like two lovers whispering. A conversation gloriously confusing and yet liberating all at the same time.

During those long mornings at the church in Hutchinson, I often found myself listening to myself. Something or someone who was in me was praying, on the inside, deep down in my

---

* Jean Vanier, *Becoming Human* (New York: Paulist Press, 2008), 32.

† Hugh Black, *Friendship* (Grand Rapids: Revell, 1898), 13.

soul where I could hear him. In this intimate, sacred space, the unseen became a reality. I felt a great sense of self-awareness and self-acceptance. I was discovering something authentic in my own soul. I was going deeper into a relationship.

Slowly, I could sense an intimacy that I had been missing. I became aware that he was calling me to leave my past and reach forward to a new way of being and living. He was inviting me into this inexhaustible life, a gift to be received and not achieved. I know now that a healing of past disappointments and regrets was taking place deep inside my soul.

The conversation was continual and constant and consuming. I was living in a fog, a cloud of holy presence! I knew it was real, and yet I couldn't explain it to anyone.

Word got around the small congregation that the pastor was going to the sanctuary to pray every morning. Soon, the retired couples started showing up around nine in the morning, and they would stay until noon, simply supporting me and agreeing with my extemporaneous prayers. These informal prayer meetings created an atmosphere of spiritual depth and charged the building with an energy of divine love. I prayed in tongues more than I prayed in English. I was so consumed by the Holy Spirit that I'd answer the phone in tongues! I ended up downtown a couple of different times, just speaking in tongues like it was the most natural thing in the world. Good Lord, whatever happened to my grandmother is happening to me!

My overseer was a good man named Elston Page, the district superintendent for the state of Kansas for the Pentecostal Holiness church. He cared deeply for me and for my family and called two or three times a week just to check on me. He said that every time he called, the woman who answered the phone told him I was in prayer. He thought I was avoiding him, so he finally drove to Hutchinson. When he arrived, he discovered this handful of old people and their young pastor praying in the sanctuary of this little church on the corner.

I still remember his face as I tried to explain what was happening to me. I'm sure I confused him. Revelation comes into our souls on a jet plane, but understanding comes on a mule train. At least, that's how it feels to me.

"I can't seem to stop. I don't want to stop." I was babbling. "In fact, I'm trying to figure out if I need to go to a retreat center or a monastery for a few days."

I had been reading everything I could get my hands on—old and new. Much to my surprise, I began finding deep wisdom in writings by the early church fathers. Frankly, I didn't even know we had "fathers of the faith," but here they were, voices from the past, speaking into the present moment.

After listening to me babble on for a few hours, Brother Page suggested we spend more time together. He wanted me to accompany him to a conference on prayer at Larry Lea's Church on the Rock in Rockwall, Texas. Unbeknownst to me, a prayer movement was sweeping across America in the 1980s—I wasn't the only one experiencing this deep call.

Pastor Lea had written a book called *Could You Not Tarry One Hour?* He talked about getting caught up in a season of prayer so deeply that he thought he'd lost his mind. He validated my experience in prayer. I wasn't losing my mind. What a relief! The entire focus of the conference was on praying the Lord's Prayer. Most Pentecostals prayed extemporaneously—many of the conference attendees might have found the idea of repeating a prayer not only novel but somehow less spiritual.

Unlike my denominational tribesmen, my time in the basement of Christ Lutheran had given me a deep appreciation for the Lord's Prayer.

Years before, Father O'Connor had handed me the Anglican prayer book, *The Book of Common Prayer*, and said, "When your passion wanes, your discipline will sustain. Keep this close." The Lord's Prayer and the structure of the prayer book, in harmony with my Pentecostal hunger, came crashing together in a wonderful way. I was discovering the convergence of old and new. The combination of an "old" prayer saturated in "new" wine was exhilarating. I felt like I had discovered a mysterious secret.

I was experiencing unfiltered goodness unmitigated by anyone else. Thomas Aquinas taught that God is happiness. "God's happiness, as Thomas sees it, is the friendship life that is God; it is this everlasting community of friendship love that we call Trinity."*

This season of prayer was when I begin to live in true friendship with God. The mere idea that he had chosen me was intoxicating, and that intoxication was amplified in our conversations, which had little to do with the circumstances of life. In this collision between charismatic manifestation and quiet contemplation, I was experiencing real communion, unlike anything I thought possible. The more I was willing to receive and respond to his friendship, the more he confirmed my identity as a beloved son. I could not stop! Nor did I try.

Any and all conversation with the Lord ultimately leads to thanksgiving. Suddenly, I was thankful for everything that had

---

* Paul J. Wadell, C.P., *Friendship and the Moral Life* (Notre Dame: University of Notre Dame Press, 1994).

ever happened—every disappointment and every challenge seemed like a gift. Every friend I'd ever had was a gift from God. Every bit of it had been preparatory—stepping-stones to this moment of communion in which I expressed my gratitude to God. Annie and I both realized how God had orchestrated our lives. I couldn't say thank you enough.

Annie and I had lost everything. When Dad died, the business died. Everything that he had ever dreamed for the family died. Our home, our hopes, my family—they all seemed to have been blown away by that cold December wind. Here we were, living with three small children in a pair of box cars pushed together. We were broke, but we were thankful. Thankful for the opportunity to serve. Thankful for every one of those twenty-two people who believed in us.

The Lutheran theologian Albert Schweitzer said, "The greatest thing is to give thanks for everything. He who has learned this knows what it means to live. He has penetrated the whole mystery of life: giving thanks for everything."* Thankfulness requires training, and I was in bootcamp. I was learning the apostle Paul's glorious lesson: "I have learned to be satisfied in any circumstance. I know what it means to lack, and I know what it means to experience overwhelming abundance. For I'm trained in the secret of overcoming all things." (Phil. 4:11-13, TPT)

As Abundant Life Church sought the Lord in prayer, many people began to sincerely ask for the Lord's forgiveness. More

* Albert Schweitzer, *Reverence for Life*, translated by Reginald H. Fuller (New York: Harper, 1969), 41.

than once, Annie and I listened to people as they faced their past failures. We prayed with them and wept with them. Many lives were changed as people worked through their humanity. Annie and I continually sought the Lord's guidance to know how to love and nurture these people the Lord was bringing into our lives.

We continually felt impressed that the Lord was telling us, "Cover them with grace." If there is one thing that I am even more confident about today, it is the power of his grace. I truly believe that his grace is sufficient.

Sometimes these congregants would have a clear leading from the Holy Spirit about something they needed to do or someone with whom they needed to make amends. Sometimes they simply had to work through their sins without burdening others with their past issues. On more than one occasion, folks asked me whether they needed to do something besides repent. Each situation seemed personal and sacred to us. There wasn't one formula that fit every individual. Years later, I realized that the Lord was sanctifying our lives with his mercy.

Meanwhile, certain people within our regional conference of churches wanted certain issues made public. Though I was vaguely aware of the politics, I didn't much care what they thought. However, when Jesse Doyle Simmons, the evangelism director for the denomination, called, I thought I was in trouble.

"Quintin, Lady Lois and I would just love to come up and be in service with you," said Brother Simmons. He had this great South Carolina drawl. "We've heard so much about what's happening there, and it sounds exciting."

We set a date for his visit, and I instantly began to worry.

J. D. Simmons, who had ordained me into the Pentecostal

Holiness church, had pastored for years in South Carolina before moving to Oklahoma City where the denomination was headquartered. He dressed in the most beautiful suits—they were never wrinkled. Everything about him spoke of a formal Southern preacher. His wife, Lady Lois, was one of the sweetest people I've ever met.

I will never forget his opening line, mostly because of its impact on my soul, but also because he sang it, and he couldn't sing.

"I AM A SON OF GOD! YOU ARE SONS OF GOD!"

The apostle Paul wrote, "But when the time arrived that was set by God the Father, God sent his Son, born among us of a woman, born under the conditions of the law so that he might redeem those of us who have been kidnapped by the law. Thus, we have been set free to experience our rightful heritage. You can tell for sure that you are now fully adopted as his own children because God sent the Spirit of his Son into our lives crying out, 'Papa! Father!'" (Galatians 4:4-7, MSG)

That day, our small fellowship was released from the bondage of performance. Brother Simmons brought into the open our identity in Christ. No longer slaves, but children of God. The walls of shame-based spirituality so entrenched in our religious experience crumbled a bit more.

Brother Simmons not only preached about sonship, but he also treated me as a son. He became like a father not only to me but to the whole church. Over the next twenty years, well into his retirement, he visited and offered us direction or simply called me to spend time with him. I am humbled by his love and will forever honor our friendship. This denominational leader risked many things to encourage a young pastor to continue stretching beyond the biases of our denomination's particular doctrines.

After service, sitting in my office, he looked at me as if he were peering into my soul. "Son, all I want to know is what the Lord has spoken to you."

Without hesitation, I said, "Brother Simmons, all I keep hearing the Lord say is, 'Cover them with grace.'"

I'll never forget his smile as he said, "Son, don't ever stop!"

During this season of prayer and thanksgiving, I began serving communion. By all standards, the setup wasn't very liturgical, but I tried to model it as best I could from my Lutheran experience. When people professed faith in Jesus, I found a place to baptize them. I now realize I was living a blended reality, bringing together the scriptures, the sacraments, and the Holy Spirit, though I didn't have a good understanding or language for what I was doing.

At the same time, the church began to grow. The church didn't just grow—it downright exploded. We were adding new people to the congregation every Sunday until, by June of 1987, we'd blossomed from our original twenty-two members to 150 regular attendees.

God's mercy and love were so present. All I wanted to do was share this wonderful goodness I was experiencing. All anyone needed to know was his love and grace. Though that may sound simplistic, it's what I believed and still do. Teenagers no one else would accept flooded our church. Restless to serve the Lord, a few zealous teenagers and I began walking the streets of South Hutchinson. Many of these teenagers came from broken homes. I often heard them say, "My mom and dad don't want me." Or, "Nobody wants me." Together, we discovered many other broken and often homeless people who had been ignored and overlooked by city officials. Refugees of darkness! My heart broke for these people. Now I knew what the Lord meant all those years ago. He wasn't talking about refugees of some distant war but rather refugees of our society's darkness—the outcasts, the outsiders, the lost, those whom nobody else wanted.

I knew we were meant to reach out and embrace these people God had led us to.

When I shared my heart with my congregation, they joined me in praying, "God, send us everybody no one else wants!" God continues to faithfully answer this one prayer. I was in love with Jesus, and I was in love with his people—even the unruly, unwanted misfits of church and society. A few years ago, a friend of mine described our church as "The Island of Misfit Toys," an appropriate moniker.

Soon after the teenagers came gang members with their long hair, body piercings, and tattoos. One Sunday morning, a man named John made his way down to the front of the church. John was six-foot-two with a head full of dreadlocks and clothing dating from the sixties. He smelled bad and hadn't shaved in years. Once upon a time, he'd been a regular guy, a professional, before he lost his wife. He'd been living in his car in Kingman, Kansas, when one of the street teens who attended our services ran into him and invited him to church.

When I saw John headed down the aisle, I thought he was going to sit on the front row. Instead, he sat down cross-legged on the floor before the first pew. He smiled at me, and I continued with my sermon. But no one was listening—all eyes were on Brother Lawrence, one of the founding members of the church. Seeing John there on the floor, he stood up from his seat. At seventy-two, he didn't move as swiftly as he once did. He walked to the front of the church and slowly lowered himself down beside John.

Our community changed that day. We truly meant what we had been praying—our church had opened its door and our hearts to accept the unacceptable and to love the unlovable.

Soon, gypsies began streaming in, family by family. I thought gypsies were something from the movies—I had no idea there was an entire subculture of them in the United States. These nomadic Romani folks worked hard in the community—they painted barns or paved driveways or cleared pastures, any number of odd jobs. Several times their communities in remote corners of the country brought me in to speak to them at local gatherings.

Bikers—and I mean, real bikers—began to show up, members of the Sons of Silence. I didn't know we were supposed to be concerned. I didn't know they were gangs on wheels. All I knew to do was love them.

In the fall of 1992, I met Eugene "High Side," a leader in a local Sons of Silence group who came to church dressed in black leather and chaps. He got his nickname because every time he wrecked his bike, he walked away—he came out on the "high side." His wife, Lonna, had attended a women's conference at our church where she ended up baptized in the Holy Spirit. She soon started attending regularly. The day High Side attended our service, he gave his heart to the Lord and later became the first chaplain in his outlaw biker gang.

Another member of High Side's motorcycle gang, Bob "Rat," came to Christ and asked to be baptized. He stood six feet tall with hair down to his waist and a beard that reached his belt buckle. As Rat stepped down into the water, still dressed in his black leather pants and boots, he laid his knives and a pistol on the edge of the baptistry.

"Do you know Jesus as your Lord?" A simple question.

"I do now, pastor." A simple answer.

"Do you understand what we're doing?" I asked.

"Yeah—you're gonna bury me in water, and when I'm raised up, I'll be a new man."

"I'm honored to call you brother," I said, moved to tears. "I will be here for you as you step into your identity as a son of God."

Besides weapons like those carried by the Sons of Silence, I soon realized addicts were leaving behind their particular belongings in the prayer room. We held a board meeting to decide how to dispose of the heroin, needles, marijuana, and pipes. That still happens in our church today. God sends us those no one else will tolerate because we receive them with open arms, just as they are.

Despite outward appearances, what we all had in common was a need for true connection. I remember the moment I met Tim. "I don't need a pastor or a prophet or healer—I need a friend," he said.

His wife was in the final stages of cancer. He had two little children. He needed someone to listen, someone who didn't have all the answers. He had come to the right guy, as I had no clue what to tell him, but we could love him, and that's what we did. The day we laid his wife to rest turned into a poignant celebration. It was painful to help him take those first few steps, but he became one of my dearest friends. His journey and mine will forever be intertwined.

Hidden in this midwestern Kansas town, a community of people were allowing the Holy Spirit to lead them into an authentic expression of the Christian faith. We were focusing our desire on the "one thing necessary," to sit at the feet of Jesus. We were discovering the freedom to live from our heart's desire for him. We were stumbling out of the grasp of the restrictive paradigms of shallow religion.

The church seemed to explode in growth long before I had ever heard of "church growth techniques." I had no idea why they were coming, but they did. Perhaps it was the prayer for acceptance or the willingness to be personal. Maybe it was the collision of traditions that I didn't realize was uncommon. These converging elements created a healthier environment conducive to people discovering Christ and being transformed. We created a spiritual atmosphere free of fear and shame so people could truly grow.

We encountered a tsunami of people hungry for something fresh. Some were Protestant; others were Catholic. Some were Pentecostals; others were Baptists. All of us were seekers and followers of Christ. In the midst of our newfound authenticity, we realized that it was nearly impossible to seek the divinity of God without honoring the essential dignity of every human being. Broken lives continued to fill our little sanctuary—lives changed by the glorious presence of a loving God who gave them a hope and a future. People searching for a sense of value and identity wept at the altar week after week. I was so young and inexperienced that all I knew to do was to pray and weep with them.

We navigated the magnetic pull of cultural accommodation, and we tried not to drown in the growing political pull of the times. We simply prepared the way of the Lord by providing an atmosphere of unconditional love *where every person could discover Christ, become a disciple of Christ, and be deployed to their highest potential in Christ.* We were radically Christian—we loved Jesus, we loved people, and we truly wanted to make a difference in our community and the world. We were compelled to reach everyone with the news that they were loved unconditionally. I clearly remember the prayer from Isaiah: "I will say to the north, 'Give them up!' And to the south, 'Do not keep them back!' Bring My sons from afar, and My daughters from the ends of the earth." (Isaiah 43:6) And they did.

When I first arrived at Abundant Life, our sanctuary held only a hundred people. By June of 1987, we were fifty people over capacity. Knowing I had a background in construction, the elders asked me to build them a new building. Funny that I was both a carpenter and a pastor. I like to say I've worked for just two carpenters my whole life—my dad and Jesus. In the fall of 1988, we finished building our new church—a beautiful corner sanctuary set at a triangle with an increased capacity of up to 250 people. The new building included offices, and we connected it to another old metal structure on the property that we renovated for classrooms.

But by the end of 1991, we were running two services on Sunday mornings and packed out each time. Once again, we gutted the building to expand the sanctuary and moved the offices and Sunday School classes into two houses across the street.

I was learning by trial and error (mostly error). I was devouring every book I could find and listening to every sermon possible. I had come to understand that all of us needed to see our story with new eyes. Subconsciously, we all have particular biases. We come to conclusions about God, other people, and ourselves that aren't actually true. Far too many people limit God to something defined by their own experience. If unchallenged, the story we've been telling ourselves will block the flow of God's blessing.

I found myself telling people, "Give me a year. If you will listen, God's grace and mercy will make huge changes in the way you see and experience life. Life is so much more than what you think or what you've been told. Life is a mystery that must be embraced without the boundaries of your limited imagination. Together, we will find a sacred imagination that will open our eyes to that which is above and beyond. Abundant life is available to all of us."

Everyone in our church was recovering from something, an addiction, a divorce, or a trauma. Everyone had reason to distrust religion, to find God suspect. But we were thankful for grace. We were learning the secret of thanksgiving. We were beginning to trust in the One who chose us—he who is good, all the time.

CHAPTER 7

Beyond Hutchinson

> "Whenever you did one of these things to someone overlooked or ignored, that was me—you did it to me."
>
> —Jesus (Matthew 25:40, MSG)

I will never forget the moment that Brother Simmons looked at me and said, "God has called you to more than Hutchinson."

Because he recognized something in me, in 1989, he sent me to London where the Pentecostal Holiness denomination had a school near Finsbury Park. The Centre for International Christian Ministries received students from all over the world—England, India, Hong Kong, Philippines, Korea, Croatia, Sweden, Mexico, Nigeria, Ghana, Ivory Coast, Kenya, Uganda, Tanzania, Zimbabwe, South Africa, and many more.

Don Thomas and Harold Presley evangelized people on the streets of Finsbury Park and other neighborhoods of London, and those who were interested were enrolled in the missions school. The vision was to plant churches around the world, and it worked. Countless missionaries were sent back to their countries, and numerous churches were planted.

Though Brother Simmons was, in no small way, responsible for my love for missions, it was Glenn Edmonds, a friend from the Hutchinson congregation, who first pushed me to take real action the year before. Glenn lived fifty miles away in Wichita, but his father-in-law was one of the founders of Abundant Life many years prior.

"Quintin, I have friends in Monterey you need to meet," said Glenn. The Lord has always brought me people who wanted to introduce me to their friends.

I'm pretty sure Glenn had the Mexican flag tattooed somewhere on his body, such was his love for the country. He drove me nuts until I finally agreed to go with him on a mission trip over Thanksgiving of 1988. I ignored him as long as I could—I had no real desire to go. But then he convinced ten people to give him $350 each to cover our travel expenses, and we were on our way.

About a dozen of us traveled together from Kansas. Glenn planned for us to leave the Tuesday afternoon before Thanksgiving and drive from Kansas to San Rafael, a small high-desert community situated in the municipality of Galeana, Nuevo León. Most of the 3,000 people who live in the little town work as sharecroppers on surrounding farms, growing corn, wheat, potatoes, tomatoes, and apples, among other things.

Glenn loaded those vans and trailers with every conceivable item he thought anyone would use. Twenty-five hours in one direction, a horrible drive. The entire way, he kept telling me I was going to meet people who would become friends for life.

We arrived in San Rafael late at night. All I remember was not having a good time on the way down. But early on Thanksgiving morning, I woke up in a simple, four-room home filled with love for Jesus and for people. Glenn and I sat around an old stove on which two missionaries, Octavio and Adricola, cooked tortillas and laughed about our drive down. Sister Adricola didn't speak much English, and we spoke no Spanish, but we understood each other perfectly.

César Octavio Lara Cepeda and Adricola Reyes de Lara had been pastoring the Good Shepherd Church for more than seventy years. During their ministry, they had opened many churches in the surrounding villages—riding in a wagon drawn by oxen to reach the villagers.

After breakfast, Adricola invited us to walk to the church. As I stepped off the curb into the street, I felt like I had stepped into flour. With every step, a cloud of fine dust rose from my feet. By the time we had walked half a block, this cloud of dust had filled the street. I had no idea how long it had been since this town last saw rain. I began to cry.

Glenn Edmonds had introduced me to Judy, an International Pentecostal Holiness missionary to Mexico since the early sixties. Though she lived in Monterrey, Judy hosted our group in San Rafael. She turned to me and said, "If the dust of Mexico gets in your heart, you'll never be able to leave."

Her words were prophetic in more ways than one.

On the evening of Thanksgiving, Octavio drove his pickup truck into the country to find families who wanted to come to church. His truck bed, which was covered with a tarp, filled up with mostly young children. The air was cold, and it began to snow ever so lightly, but the flakes didn't deter anyone from hopping on board.

In the small sanctuary, everywhere I looked I saw tiny faces. Some were shy, but all of them were smiling. We waited as he made trip after trip. Around 8:30 p.m., Adricola began playing guitar. She didn't have a guitar pick, so she borrowed a pink comb from one of the little girls. She sat on the platform and sang with the passion of a rock musician—the best worship service I've ever experienced. The people sang loud and long. They lifted their hands and gave thanks for all that God had provided. They cried, unashamed.

Adricola motioned for me to stand up and preach, but I had nothing to say. All I could do was think of how grateful I was. Grateful to be in this place. Grateful for the opportunity to love these people. I was so spoiled, so self-centered. They were giving to me, not the other way around.

In San Rafael, I began to learn that evangelism is based entirely on friendship. There is no way to fulfill the Great Commission if the greatest commandment—to love God and your neighbor—has not been written on your heart. Friendship is the living out of the love of God. There is no program that can replace helping those you love. Jesus tells us to go make disciples—I think my translation would read "go make friends."

The walls of my heart were crumbling that night in San Rafael. The borders of my mind were being breached. I couldn't stop crying for these children, and after three decades, I'm still weeping—not only for the children in San Rafael but for every child in need of food and water, shelter and clothing. And most of all, in need of the gospel of love—a love that doesn't merely pray but takes action. Love unlimited by denominational division, cultural accommodation, or political partisanship. Love that breaks the barrier of human logic and simply recognizes the value of every human being. Glenn was right that I needed to meet his friends. It was my privilege to have these people call me their friend and brother—they helped shape my life in ways I never thought possible, and they gave me more than I ever gave them.

Today in America, we are constantly being told that we need to protect ourselves from those living south of the border. Don't talk to me about building walls to keep out immigrants—I've spent thirty years of my life loving on these people made in the image of God. Nothing frustrates me more than those who treat them like political pawns. We think these people are a threat. I agree they are a threat. They threaten our selfishness. They threaten our arrogance. They threaten our bigotry. They threaten our way of living, one that isolates us from the needs of others. They threaten our shallow understanding of the gospel. If we ignore them, we ignore Christ.

I will never forget the verse that came to my heart that night in San Rafael: "Sons are a heritage from the Lord, children a reward from him. Like arrows in the hands of a warrior are sons born in one's youth. Blessed is the man whose quiver is full of them. They will not be put to shame when they contend with their enemies in the gate." (Psalm 127:3-5, NIV)

I laid hands on every child in the room that night, and I wept over each of them. I prayed for them, knowing they would change their generation somehow. They simply needed a friend to help. As I finally dozed off to sleep that night, I could hear the rain begin to fall—it was a sign!

Many of those same children ended up attending a Bible

school that I helped rebuild in Monterrey with another native named Juan Carlos Lopez. Juan pastored a city church in downtown Monterrey called Open Door Church. During a subsequent trip to Mexico the following spring, the place was packed out. The building was an engineering nightmare—a tragedy waiting to happen. Four-by-four posts stuck around the room held up the second floor. I now realize that I was seeing an image of a church in need of repair, as Saint Francis of Assisi was called to do. Cheap fans hung around the side walls trying unsuccessfully to circulate the stuffy air. They didn't help much—they just turned the 110 degrees into an even hotter furnace. But the congregants sang and sang and sang, a sound from heaven. Lots of young people had come to Monterrey to find work and a better life. Full of hope and promise, they exuded an electric faith.

Pastor Juan looked twenty years older than he was—life had been difficult, and he suffered from health issues. He had scratched and bled for his congregation, and not only them—he'd also ministered all over Latin America and even Cuba. I loved the rancheros in San Rafael, but Juan and I became covenant brothers. I liked him and wanted to be involved in whatever he was doing, whether in Mexico or other parts of Latin America.

"Pastor Quiiinnntin," he said, drawing out my name as he spoke, "I want to give you this coin to symbolize our brotherhood. I have never met an American who loves the Mexican people more than you. You bring more than just things to us—you bring us unconditional love. And you bring us hope that others will see beyond the color of our skin and recognize we are their brothers. You have been called a preacher, a teacher, and a prophet, but today I say that you are a 'sower of love.' Every time you look at this coin, I want you to remember that you and I are covenant brothers, friends forever."

Juan and I went on to work together on refurbishing and revitalizing a Bible school in Monterrey. My congregation and I poured tens of thousands of dollars into the project. Through other relationships, I accessed training materials from a missions school in Tulsa, Oklahoma. Juan and I took that material and turned it into a nine-month curriculum for the school in Monterrey. What I didn't realize at the time was that relationship would one day lead to another connection that would open up a whole other part of the world to me.

Many of the teenage rancheros from San Rafael attended this Bible school, and throughout the late 1980s until 1996, we helped many of them plant more than seventy churches throughout Mexico and Guatemala, as well as three clandestine churches in Cuba that went on to spawn many more.

During that season, I spent about one week a month in Mexico raising up teachers and church leaders. Juan and I continued to labor together to see the Bible school thrive. Our children became close friends, just as we had, and our churches paralleled on so many levels, reflecting a truly unique friendship. That first mission trip to San Rafael that Thanksgiving more than thirty years ago altered the entire course of my journey.

Juan had called me a "sower of love." My church's love for missions continued to increase, and soon we founded Sowers of Love International, which facilitated short-term mission trips and assisted with a multitude of projects. In the early 1990s, we saw an opportunity to reach the former Soviet Union with the gospel. Our strategy was to partner our US-based church with a group of people from USSR and the Ukraine in order to assist them with planting a church. Teams from our church made several trips to the former USSR to help at least three such churches—an unforgettable experience.

During that season, I heard about a man named Daniel Williams from Calvary International based out of Florida. He had developed a strategy for planting thousands of churches in Europe—truly an amazing endeavor. Everywhere I looked, ministries were focused on evangelizing the world. Daniel and I were on a path that would converge in a matter of years.

In 1992, I kept having the same vivid dream night after night. I was surrounded by Latin American people singing and shouting their praises to the Lord, but I wasn't in Mexico or Guatemala. The faces were different—next to the Latin American faces were some that looked almost European, while others looked Native American. I saw myself praying for person after person. I knew I was being drawn to them. I would wake up with a sense of urgency to help, but I didn't know what to do.

One afternoon, I was sitting in my office when our receptionist informed me that a gentleman from a group called Pastors for Peace was on the phone. Pastors for Peace is a special ministry of the Interreligious Foundation for Community Organization created in 1988 to deliver humanitarian aid to Latin America and the Caribbean. In 1992, Pastors for Peace began organizing "Friendshipment" caravans to Cuba.

I will never forget what the person on the other end of the phone said to me: "We have heard of your work in Mexico and wanted to know if you would join us in helping the Cuban people."

At the time, their strategy was to fill school buses with all kinds of materials and aid that would be valuable to Cubans. Churches from all over the country participated. About forty-two buses drove to Montreal and were loaded onto barges that traveled down the Atlantic Ocean along the eastern coast to deliver those items.

I was so moved by this project that I began making inquiries about going to Cuba myself. It took several months to make contacts and gain some kind of assurances that we would be able to enter Cuba and return. The International Pentecostal Holiness Church had had churches in Cuba before 1958 whose leaders we were able to contact. We prayed for weeks before we were given visas (much to the dissatisfaction of the US State Department). Under a great prayer covering, a small group of several Pentecostal pastors took off for Havana to meet with pastors from every denomination imaginable—Methodists, Baptists, Pentecostals, Anglicans, Nazarenes. This diverse group of believers smiled and welcomed our small group of pastors from the US.

My host, Brother Castillio, was excited to explain that in Cuba the churches all worked together—there was no division among the believers because they had to rely on each other. Brother Castillio had been incarcerated many times for his faith. During his imprisonment, other ministers cared for his churches and his family. We stayed in a Methodist retreat center and ministered in several different denominational churches.

One church stood out to me more than the others, a small room twenty-five feet wide and maybe seventy-five feet long. There were no benches or chairs because they took up too much room. A praise band played at one end, powered by car batteries that also powered the two light bulbs in the room, which flickered when the music got loud. The people sang praise and worship for over an hour, covering the floor with perspiration. When I asked about the sweat, Brother Castillio smiled and said that the Lord had told them he would rain on Cuba again. They truly believed that their worship was bringing the promise of deliverance.

As I stood up to preach, I realized that the dream I had been dreaming for several years was taking place in real life—here before me were all of those different faces. All I could do was weep. The more I wept, the more they wept. The more we wept, the more the power of the Lord moved through that room. People fell to the floor. Children with club feet were healed. The presence of the Lord was beyond anything I've ever witnessed. Cubans hadn't had any dental health care for years, but a phenomenon had begun long before I arrived. Brother Castillio referred to it as the "great fall and the great filling." He explained that, for several years when people fell out under the power of the Spirit, they got back up with their cavities filled—*with gold*. I saw it with my own eyes.

Years later, Brother Castillio came to Kansas and gave his testimony to our church, which was one of the most encouraging moments in the life of our congregation. We weren't just supporting missions; we were all involved in reaching the world with the good news of Christ. The more we were involved in missions abroad, the more the church grew at home. The greatest commandment and the Great Commission are uniquely connected in the kingdom of God.

In Cuba, I began to understand that the unity of the church was key to the evangelization of the world. When the church works across its self-imposed boundaries, both governmentally and denominationally, the kingdom of God will be made manifest on earth. Though it would take years for me to be able to implement this revelation in my local setting, I'm forever grateful for the deposit that the beautiful people of Cuba made in my life. Many churches were born out of that season. I'm so humbled to have been a small part of that movement. Pastors for Peace continue their great ministry of leading people to not only Cuba but other parts of the world.

We all have heard those stories, some funny and some not so funny, about taking public prayer requests. Today, in lieu of prayer requests, we film testimonies, which is a whole lot less risky. Far too often the prayer requests involved too much history and not enough mystery. Can I get an amen? Thank God, now we show videos. One Sunday morning during service, however, a young man named Wayne raised his hand and asked us to pray for his dad, Harold Nichols.

I knew the name sounded familiar, but it didn't register until I started delivering my sermon. Then, a voice went off in my head so loud I stopped in mid-sentence. "Your dad is Harold Nichols?" (Did I say that out loud?)

"Yes!" he said.

I finished the message, but God only knows if it made any sense. Harold Nichols was Kenneth Copeland's pastor for life. Kenneth Copeland is a charismatic preacher of the Word of Faith movement and one of the most-watched television preachers of the late twentieth century. He captivated audiences by proclaiming the power of a word spoken in faith to lay claim on blessings, healing, and prosperity from the hand of God.

Who would have guessed that this church in Hutchinson, Kansas, would have a connection to a famous television preacher? Harold Nichols's son Wayne had married a woman named Jill who had grown up in a small community not far from Hutchinson. She had a degree in broadcasting from Oral Roberts University, where she had met Terri Copeland, Kenneth's daughter. Jill and Terry were on the team that put together his broadcasting crew. Never in my wildest dreams would I have thought there would be a connection to someone so well-known.

Over the next few months, Annie and I were invited to a few small gatherings in Texas where we met not only Kenneth Copeland but also his friend Jerry Savelle, a fellow evangelist who has spent a lot of his life involved in foreign missions.

At that time, everyone in charismatic or Pentecostal circles knew of Jerry Savelle. He was a pivotal figure in the Word of Faith movement whose message was spreading rapidly all over America and the world. I invited Brother Jerry to Hutchinson, but he declined—he didn't know me very well, and I wasn't quick enough to pick up on his vetting process. He suggested that his wife, Carolyn, would enjoy coming to lead a women's meeting. Carolyn was an absolute joy, and the women loved her. We all had a great time.

As we dropped her off at the airport, she said, "I think Len Mink should come next."

All I knew about Len was that he was a worship leader who led the praise service for Brother Copeland's Southwest Believers' Convention. Len is a wonderful man. He tells the story of how he had a successful career in broadcasting and yet was depressed. He had interest in Buddhism, but he hadn't found any real peace until he accepted Christ. The first time I met him, I realized he was one of the happiest men I had ever met. He sang with this beautiful voice and then pulled out "Gospel Duck," a puppet that entertained the children (and everyone else) with singing and a discussion of what it meant to be in a relationship with Jesus.

When Len was on his way out, he turned to me and said, "I think Jerry will come if you ask him again."

And he did. Promoting Jerry's appearance at Abundant Life Church was a piece of cake. The early 1990s were the golden age of television evangelism, and Jerry Savelle had appeared on Kenneth Copeland's program Believer's Voice of Victory many times. Everyone in our tribe seemed to know who Brother Jerry was. Our building had seating for four hundred people, and we set up the gym with video streaming as an overflow area. We had no idea what was about to happen.

Cars jammed the streets leading to the church. We broke every building code possible, and people still kept coming. Before the evening ended, we counted more than nine hundred people. That era was truly an amazing time in our country—everyone was hungry for teachings on faith.

That night, Brother Jerry taught about the unmerited favor of God. Each of us is God's favorite child, not because we earned it, but because of his love for us. He claimed favor on our lives because of God's love for each of us. Brother Jerry's message of favor bolstered our faith in God's grace and unconditional love, freeing us anew from the lingering legalism of shame-based spirituality.

A subconscious idea had lingered in my mind since childhood. If someone had too much financial success, then they must have compromised their faith. I thought that the less you had, the holier you were. That night, Jerry Savelle revealed that God's favor rested on all of us and God wants to bless us. The hardest thing to do in life is to accept the favor of God. Why? Because you know you don't deserve it; that's why it's called favor. I didn't have to be poor to be holy! Religious people have a strong tendency to swing from one extreme to the other, especially as it pertains to this subject.

In the early nineties, there was a revival of prayer, praise, and scripture. People wanted to learn. I wanted to learn. We wanted to understand how Jesus lived and how his life affected our lives today. Straightforward teaching, free of denominational restraints. It was a glorious time. Radical Christians who believed that God was the same today as yesterday.

Jerry later introduced me to Jesse Duplantis, a highly successful evangelist. Jerry and Jesse came together several times, and we filled the Hutchinson Sports Arena with several thousand people, many of whom drove from several states away to hear the word of God. Throughout the early 1990s, Jerry and Jesse preached in my church numerous times. During this season, our church hosted a number of other nationally known speakers and artists. This small community of friends became a hub of impressive speakers and artists making an impact on the Midwest.

In 1994, Brother Jerry invited me to travel with him to Africa. We flew to Nairobi, Kenya, to teach at a conference held at the Kenyatta Center, an auditorium that seats up to nine thousand people. Nairobi is a long way from Severy, Kansas. I was in awe—I still am! That Wednesday morning, I arrived to find two thousand attendees ready for the daytime sessions. Jerry asked if I'd be willing to teach that morning.

For my sermon, I spoke about the death of a promise—God makes promises but then waits until it seems impossible for the promise to come to pass. Death rolls in until all seems hopeless. He promised Abraham he would be the father of many nations, but Abraham wakes up one day—he's eighty-six, and his wife, Sarah, is no spring chicken either. He takes Hagar as a surrogate wife and has a son named Ishmael—that wasn't God's plan. God waits until Abraham is ninety-nine before fulfilling the promise. In the gospels, Mary and Martha's brother, Lazarus, dies before Jesus could arrive to heal him. Martha tells Jesus he's too late, but Jesus calls Lazarus forth from the grave.

I had a litany of such examples. Too often, we lose patience and give up on the dream. But God will give us a promise and then remove all the ways and means by which it can be fulfilled in the natural. Then, he shows up when there is no way we can take credit for what happens. The hard part is the wait, and that is suffering. How do you live in the seasons of life when it looks like God isn't even there?

The entire hour, Dr. Savelle just stared at me. Uh, oh, I thought. But when I descended the stage, he asked, "Do you have a part two to that?"

"Yes, sir," I said.

So, I taught two hours that morning. That was the beginning of a great relationship. I traveled with Dr. Savelle quite frequently when he was an evening keynote speaker, and I was one of his morning teachers.

Our friends determine so much of who we are and who we become. God passes his gifts and anointing from person to person. Everything in the history of our faith indicates that God works through relationships to bring us into our highest and fullest potential.

My friendship with Brother Jerry released an anointing in me that I would never have otherwise known. He saw the best in me and, by that fact, called forth the best from within me. I grew up feeling completely insecure and unsure that I mattered. I certainly didn't believe I could make a difference in anyone else's life. It took the love of friends like Pat, Pete, Annie, and Jerry to find my voice and speak confidently. Jerry made me believe I could do anything—I could hop on a plane and speak on the world stage. Anything I wanted to do, I could do. My journey of faith has been facilitated by friendships—friends who have seen the best in me and called forth God's blessing upon my life.

But my deepest desire was to continue ushering hurting people into the real presence of God.

We've all heard stories about chance meetings—when people encounter each other under the most unlikely of circumstances. A chance meeting is where the paths of two strangers intersect for any number of reasons and the groundwork of a relationship is set down. In my own life, these chance meetings have resulted in job opportunities, the discovery of a favorite vacation spot, an invitation to speak, a book recommendation that changed the way I think, and more than one new friend.

From 1995 until around 2005, I traveled with Jerry Savelle and others to several countries in Africa, a geographical route that would change the trajectory of my life in myriad ways. On one of these trips, I met a British man named Tony Palmer. Tony came to Christ as a young man in South Africa. Immediately afterward, he and his wife, Emiliana, felt compelled to share the gospel of Jesus with each of their neighbors.

"Before we went out in the morning to do this door-to-door evangelization," recounted Tony, "we used to watch this crazy Texan preach the gospel—a guy named Kenneth Copeland. He used to be our encourager every morning."

Tony eventually went to work for Kenneth Copeland Ministries in South Africa, and I traveled there with Jerry Savelle. No one could have set this up. Tony and I had an instant respect for each other. Once again, we were friends of friends brought together by the common cause of the gospel of Christ.

We were both young and motivated to fulfill the call of God on our lives. He and I shared a love for reading and learning in general, and we weren't afraid to read beyond our respective theological tribes. We were both intrigued by the ancient writings of the church fathers. Here we were, two Word of Faith Pentecostals, radically saved, reading about the historic church. Quietly, we were discovering the purity of the church during the first three centuries after Christ's death and resurrection. We read about the episcopacy and apostolic succession and books on the Eucharist. We recognized that the presence of God wasn't based on our goose bumps but on the celebration of the death, burial, and resurrection of Christ.

Over the next several years, we engaged in conversations beyond the scope of our Word of Faith ministries. We spoke about how divided the church is by the various denominational divisions and political positions. We were careful to share our ideas, but I think we both felt safe having these conversations with each other. I'm not sure either one of us fully understood what was happening in our souls at the time, but now I realize that we were both searching for all that God wanted in our lives.

Tony planted seeds in my soul that I had no idea would become so influential. He shared with great passion how we had to work beyond our differences and recognize what Christians have in common. He became known among his friends and associates for his statement: “Division is diabolical, but diversity is divine.” Until we are able to respect our differences and focus on what holds us together, we limit our ability to experience new friends.

At the time, I was simply enjoying a new acquaintance and our conversations. But God is always ordering our steps. Nothing truly happens just by “chance.” This I would come to see much more fully many years later.

CHAPTER 8

Preparing the Way

"It is the work of the Holy Spirit to disturb a man or institution that is become settled or stiff."

—Alec Vidler

One afternoon in early 1992, while I was sitting in Dulles Airport waiting on a flight to London, a woman I'd never met walked up to me.

"The Holy Spirit has impressed on me that I'm supposed to give you my card," she said, speaking with a lyrical Jamaican accent. "My husband, Abraham, and I are pastors in New Jersey, and I believe God has connected us for a reason. But if not, please excuse my intrusion."

With that, she walked away. Her business card said Rev. Dr. Eve Fenton. There had been a time when I would have been perplexed by such an occurrence, but they had become so common by this point that I didn't give it much thought. I put her card in my bag, boarded my plane, and forgot about the whole encounter.

Months later, the director of our women's ministry was frustrated that she hadn't found someone to speak at our upcoming women's conference. By the third time she came into my office to discuss the matter, I shared her frustration. As she was about to storm out of my office yet again, I pulled open my desk drawer, and there was Eve Fenton's business card—the woman I'd met in the airport.

"Give this lady a call," I said, "and tell her I'm the young pastor she met at the airport outside of DC."

I was out of town the weekend of the women's conference, but I met Eve that Sunday morning during our church service. In the middle of delivering what I'm sure was a profound sermon (I kid, I kid), I had this impression that Eve had something to say.

"Mrs. Fenton, do you have something to share with the church?"

"Yes, but you are doing really well, and God never interrupts himself," she replied. "If anyone wants to hear what I have to say, tell them to come back this evening. I will simply postpone my flight until tomorrow."

I had no idea that the evening of October 11, 1992, would be another defining moment for me and our community. Sunday night attendance was usually about half of the morning service attendance, but that night, the sanctuary was packed. Eve walked back and forth across the platform, addressing the audience with fervor.

"The word of the Lord is coming to you as a people: 'Prepare me a way. Make a way for me. I want to infiltrate and penetrate this area, and I want you to make me a way. You think you are in a wilderness, but you are not. You have been prepared for this time. Every valley shall be filled. Every mountain and hill shall be brought low. The crooked way shall be made straight. The rough places shall be made smooth. All flesh shall see the glory of the Lord! Make me a high road. I want in!'

"Don't be afraid! Listen to his voice—his word has come to you. He is going to bless you with a lot of people. When they begin to come into your congregation, don't be afraid. They will come in sick, and they will leave healed. They will come in friendless, and they will leave with friends. They will come in distraught, and they will leave with confidence.

"Make the Lord a way. Keep the court of the Gentiles open—be a church of hospitality. When they come in, they're gonna look as though they don't want to be here. They will have a look on their face that says, 'Don't talk to me. The service was too long, too noisy . . . I don't like—' But don't believe it! It's all a façade, a mask. They are hurting on the inside. The Lord is saying to you, 'Reach out to them. Make me a way.' The Lord is asking you as a people to facilitate his presence. Everyone else may close down and decide to do things as usual, but he is asking you to make a way so that he can move through you to bless the people.

"When the spirit of the Lord comes to you and says, 'There will be hundreds and thousands,' don't be afraid! It is the Lord who is doing it. Don't stop to think how important you are. Don't be lifted up with pride. It's the Lord sending them in so that you can bless them with the Word and pray for them. That they may be healed. That they may be saved. That their families may be restored. So that you would teach them how to love, how to worship, how to serve.

"Remember—you are a prototype. You can't follow any other trail. There is no other pattern for what the Lord is going to be doing with you. You can't send anyone anywhere to study how. You are a prototype. You're gonna have to do it by the grace of God and a life in the spirit. Don't be afraid. The spirit of Christ Jesus will anoint you—you will lay hands on the sick.

"Some of you who are skeptical will see it with your own eyes. Anyone can believe after they see. Oh, bless the Lord—we believe before we see because we have faith. Anyone can rejoice when it's over, but it takes those with the faith of God in their heart to rejoice when the word is spoken. Let the rest rejoice after it is over—you with faith rejoice!"

Remember—you are a prototype. Those words have lingered in my soul for years. So many times, as I have wrestled with what the Lord was showing me, I could hear Eve's beautiful voice saying, "You are a prototype." She encouraged us to lean into God's presence. Though it sounded odd, if I hadn't lived through what followed, I would wonder about such a prophecy. But our church soon realized that it wasn't programs, procedures, or policies that change people's lives but the real presence of God. In his presence is fullness of joy; at his right hand are pleasures forevermore. (Psalm 16:11)

We understood that we were preparing the way of the Lord. We were making room for the Holy Spirit to work in every area of our lives. We began to live in such a way that every aspect of our lives was united to Christ. Christianity became more than a set of rules or a denomination or even a culture to accommodate. Christianity became a way of living, a call to live in his presence. We were called to prepare the way of the Lord by loving each other and the world unconditionally. Above and beyond any rules or regulations, we enjoyed relationships lived in a common mutuality that reflected the Sermon on the Mount and the great treatise on love in 1 Corinthians 13. The church became a family where every person mattered, and everyone knew it.

By 1997, I had been pastoring Abundant Life Church for a dozen years, growing it from a dying congregation to one with 650 members. Just a year or so before, we had built a new $3 million building in which we hosted two Sunday morning services, as well as an evening service. We were one of the fastest growing churches in our denomination. Not only that, but we had also planted another six churches in Kansas. God was surely on the move.

During this season, we began to believe that the church was God's—it was the father's house. I was reading about the Catholic saint Francis of Assisi, though I didn't want anyone to know it. Saint Francis felt called to repair the church. I knew that our idea of God's house needed to be repaired. In God's house are many rooms—there is room for all kinds of people. We sensed that we needed to convey the simple truth that there was room in the house for everyone. After lots of prayer, we changed the name of our church to The Father's House.

As our congregation searched for deeper and more authentic encounters with the real presence of God, leaders of our denomination began expressing their disapproval. They frowned on my blending the teachings from the charismatic movement in our church and in the Bible school in Monterrey, Mexico. The legalism of traditional Pentecostal Holiness clashed with our emerging identity. Our celebrating the Eucharist every Sunday had, for the most part, gone unnoticed, but now it was becoming a topic of discussion. In our innocence, we were moving beyond the limitations and the legalism of any particular tribe.

What most troubled my tribe was my stance on speaking in tongues. I was heavily influenced by John Wimber, the founder of the Vineyard movement. Wimber had a unique approach to charismatic gifts—while traditional Pentecostal belief held that speaking in tongues is required evidence of a person's true baptism in the Holy Spirit, Wimber believed that speaking in tongues was merely one of many gifts bestowed on believers. His teaching was a refreshing perspective for mainstream evangelicals.

When I began teaching this truth, I was killing what was a sacred cow for many of my Pentecostal peers. To declare that a person didn't have to speak in tongues as evidence of the baptism in the Holy Spirit was simply a big no-no. A wall to never, ever tear down.

My willingness to challenge the status quo made them a bit too nervous. Some felt that I should surrender my pastorate and leave the denomination. They demanded that I stop having anything to do with the Bible school in Mexico, and they made plans to bring in a new leader for the church unless I agreed to stop all of this interdenominational madness.

One afternoon, my secretary came into my office visibly shaken. "Pastor, there's a man in the lobby who says he's here to look around because he's going to be our new pastor," she said.

I knew the man—he was a good man—but he was caught in the politics of denominationalism. After a series of meetings and conversations, it became obvious that we couldn't resolve our differences. Our church had rebuilt and renovated several times over that decade, and during this last round, I had cosigned the loan from the bank.

"If you want to take over, fine," I said. "Just take my name off of the loan, and it's all yours."

But the denomination didn't want that debt. For better or worse, that debt kept me in the pulpit and among the congregation I loved so deeply, though the Bible school and the churches into which we had poured our lives was lost to us. To this day, I still say I never left my denomination—they left me. I didn't want to leave, but they wouldn't allow me to grow beyond our limited theology.

Three years later, Simon Chan wrote, "For too long Pentecostals have been trying to defend their Pentecostal distinctiveness, but often at the expense of cutting themselves from the mainstream of Christian tradition. They are afraid that by identifying too closely with the mainstream they might lose their distinctiveness. I would argue, on the contrary, that it is when Pentecostals come to see their distinctive as part of the larger tradition that they can preserve them and maintain their integrity."*

Dr. Chan's work on Pentecostalism settled my soul. I'm not ashamed of my spiritual heritage, and the Pentecostal expression of the faith of today has grown well beyond its originally prescribed boundaries.

When Jerry Savelle heard what had happened, he called and offered to come to Hutchinson. "I'll be your ministerial

---

* Simon Chan, *Pentecostal Theology and the Christian Spiritual Tradition* (New York: Sheffield Academic Press, 2000) 7.

covering," he said.

I'm so grateful for Brother Jerry—his willingness to stand with us gave me and our congregation great comfort. I wouldn't have to go it alone. I never was the independent type—throughout my faith journey and life in ministry, I've always been in search of something bigger than myself. Jerry came to Hutchinson to ordain Annie and me into his ministerial association, Heritage of Faith Ministries. For all practical purposes, I was already immersed in the Word of Faith world. I will forever be indebted to Brother Jerry for his kindness. I was honored to travel with him and teach the truths that were changing lives around the world.

I have often thought that part of my role was to fit people with a new pair of spiritual glasses. I still tell people, "Invest in yourself, and invest in your faith. Give me a year, and I will commit to your spiritual success." I'm convinced that we must begin to see ourselves as sons and daughters of God—we are no longer orphans. His love for us is unconditional, not based on our performance but on his promise to always be with us. There is no place where he is not. There is no time that we are not his children.

As the veils of religious shame and condemnation were lifted from their eyes, and as they worked to understand the "why" behind their emotions, they began to discover new paths forward. They realized that going in circles didn't always mean they were stuck. While Joshua circled Jericho, a mighty shout was building in his lungs. The faith to keep moving—even when it looks like you're going nowhere—is often greatly rewarded. It takes time to find a new sound, and generally the sound is only discovered by circling your next victory.

By the end of 1999, seven years after Eve Fenton's prophetic word over our church, the winds of heaven began to blow. As our congregation learned to trust each other and risked letting each other see our weaknesses, the unexpected happened. A habitation of the Lord's presence settled over our lives. A raw visitation. Despite Eve's prophecy, we felt completely unprepared for the full authenticity of God's presence.

I distinctly remember the moment it started. One Sunday morning, during the first service, I stopped mid-sermon, prompted by the Holy Spirit. "You can either let me preach or sing a song, or you can give your heart to the Lord," I said, "and you can do it right now."

More than fifty people stood up and walked forward to profess their faith, and we started baptizing them one by one. We had started that first morning service at eight-thirty, but we didn't end it to start the next service. We simply kept the doors open as the place filled to the brim—eight hundred people packed out the sanctuary and balcony. No one left until mid-afternoon. In all, nearly a hundred people walked the aisle that day.

For eighteen months, we found ourselves in the middle of a blazing revival.

On Sunday mornings, I wasn't sure what to do, so I simply waited for the Holy Spirit to nudge me to say or do something. I trusted his voice. I trusted his friendship. After all of these years of learning to trust and lean into each other as friends, our whole church trusted him even more. Jesus said, "No longer do I call you servants, for a servant does not know what his master is doing; but I have called you friends, for all things that I heard from My Father I have made known to you." (John 15:15) We knew and believed that he loved us and that we were his friends. We trusted him to guide us and make known to us what we needed.

Because of my exposure to the Eucharist in the Lutheran church, I had been serving communion—the Lord's Supper—for several years. At the time, we weren't formal or liturgical, but we knew that if the bread was broken and the wine was shared, Christ was present with us just as he had been with his disciples in the upper room. The mystery of the faith is found in the Eucharist. I still don't fully understand the bread and wine—I wouldn't argue with anyone about whether it becomes the literal body and blood of Christ as the Catholics say or if it's merely a symbol of Christ as the evangelicals insist. What I do know is that something happens—communion invokes the presence of the Holy Spirit.

Through the years, the Lord's Prayer had become the focal prayer of our community, and likewise, the Lord's Supper had become the guiding point of our worship. The centerpiece of worship wasn't singing or preaching but remembering the death, burial, and resurrection of the Lord Jesus Christ. We were sitting down at the table with the Lord and giving thanks. We were hearing the scriptures read and taught. We were even more aware of his presence, and his presence ministered to us all.

We weren't following any theological plan nor were we trying to become Roman Catholic, Orthodox, or Anglican. We were simply seeking God's face with innocent intent. I was naive enough to think that if Jesus told us to do something, we should just do it. We were gathering to praise our savior in song, to hear his word, and to break bread and drink wine. The scriptures, the sacraments, and the Holy Spirit were provided for our spiritual health and transformation. In the unity of all three, we were experiencing the tangible reality of Christ with us.

We didn't gather because of the latest techniques in church growth. We were more than people who wanted to be motivated to succeed in the American dream. We weren't calling people back to a certain policy; we simply wanted to be with the Lord. We knew where two or three gathered together Christ had promised to meet with us. We knew that he would always sit down upon the "mercy seat." We weren't purpose-driven but presence-drawn.

People drove for hours to attend Sunday services. I wasn't in control of anything. At times it felt awkward, and at times exhilarating. Oftentimes, I never got around to giving my prepared sermon. My message was generally woven into times of praise and worship combined with praying for people. I found myself serving communion early in the service, perhaps after only a song or two, because I understood it was the sacrament that opened the door for the real presence of the Lord into our community. The worship team played every song we knew and then new, prophetic songs. What does it sound like when God comes walking in the cool of the day? These new songs filled our hearts with joy and peace.

My weeks were filled with praying with people all day, every day. The Lord was transforming people's hearts in amazing, miraculous ways. People overcome by the Holy Spirit fell to the ground. They broke into sobs as the weights of life were lifted from them. They gave their lives to Christ. We were walking along that thin place, that place where the veil between heaven and earth was being lifted, and we were more aware of his presence. The presence of God manifested from heaven, his sheer glory permeating the atmosphere. In the middle of nowhere Kansas, a group of nobodies was reliving the book of Acts.

Though it may sound crazy, people had obvious encounters with God, seeing visions of angels, heavenly light, even Christ himself. I've waited twenty years to tell this story because I know how it sounds, but I have hundreds of witnesses to the miraculousness of this experience. Hundreds of people converted to a life of following Jesus. Many people were healed or set free of the bondages in their lives—addictions, childhood traumas, broken marriages. We began to connect people with professional counselors to help them continue working on what the Holy Spirit had initiated in their lives.

There were no cameras to televise the event, no writers from Christian magazines, no celebrities in the making—just people crying out to God. Our imaginations were being purified by his grace. In response to honest people facing the darkest places of their lives, the Light of lights shone his raw love into our hearts. Light was displacing darkness, and true formation was taking place—a restoration of things long forgotten.

The Lord kept telling me, "This is because I love you, and I love these people. I am your friend." Many times I prayed asking God as a friend to help my friend—friends helping the friends of others.

One Sunday, the service had gone on for hours. Exhausted, I left the sanctuary at three in the afternoon and went into my office to take a shower and rest. I had been napping on my couch for about an hour when someone called my name. When I opened my office door, two ushers were lying on the floor, unable to move. I could hear another usher calling me from the end of the hallway.

"We need you, pastor," he said. "There are still hundreds of people here." As I rounded the corner, I will never forget the look on his face—I wasn't sure if it was fear or panic. "They just won't leave," he said. "We need you back, but I'm not coming in. Nobody comes back out." He knew what would happen if he did, and he wanted to remain standing.

As I stepped into the sanctuary, I saw two hundred people lying on the floor. The worship leaders were still singing. As I ponder it now, I realize we were so hungry and thirsty for something real, authentic, tangible; something "above and beyond." We loved being in the presence of Jesus.

The experience felt like an answer to prayer: "Thy kingdom come, thy will be done, on earth as it is in heaven." Some would call us prophetic, but we just called it living in communion. Some would call it a revival. We knew it was a wedding—a unity of the creator with his beloved creation.

We experienced joy, pleasure, gladness, safety, refreshment, true life. We were learning to be children who trusted in our Father enough to play in his presence. "One thing I have desired of the Lord, that will I seek, that I may dwell in the house of the Lord all the days of my life, to behold the beauty of the Lord, and to inquire in His temple." (Psalm 27:4)

King David had it right in saying only "one thing" was worthy of our desire. Jesus confirmed that Mary had chosen the "one thing" necessary, and it would not be taken away. One encounter with the One who calls us friend will change everything.

CHAPTER 9

The Explosion

> "You have forgotten who you are, and so forgotten me."
>
> —Mufasa, The Lion King

In 1999, Christians were overdosing on the *Left Behind* series, though it wasn't the first time the dispensationalists had sensationalized the end of the world. I have vivid memories of "eighty-eight reasons why the rapture is coming in 1988." Those apocalyptic novels by Tim LaHaye and Jerry Jenkins scared many believers. Only adding to the general fear was Y2K, the coming "millennium bug." I knew people who were storing food and buying generators in preparation—needless to say, they were more than worried. Our capitalistic, consumerist culture was taking great advantage of the opportunity.

Sunday after Sunday, we continued to gather in God's presence. Fear gave way to faith, and people continued to trust in

Jesus. But a cloud of suspicion was growing on the horizon.

On Wednesday, January 17, 2001, everyone in town felt and heard something when downtown Hutchinson blew up. Citizens on Main Street could see that something horrible had just happened.

Undetected natural gas, seeping from underground injection wells, had silently collected under and within two downtown businesses—one a party supply store and the other a furniture shop. When that gas ignited, the explosion shattered windows down several city blocks and completely destroyed several buildings. Staff and customers staggered into the street, remarkably only dazed and shaken.

Within minutes, the two businesses were ablaze. Fire and police chiefs and crews rushed toward the sound of the explosion. The city manager headed to Hutchinson's emergency operations center and stayed there for days as the crisis unfolded.

A few miles from this initial explosion, a geyser of gas burst from the ground, spewing mud and rocks high overhead. In other places, dirty brown water broke through the earth and caught fire. Our quiet midwestern community was stunned but relieved that no one had lost their life.

But early the next day, another plume of gas and water erupted under a home in Big Chief Mobile Home Park, killing two. Hundreds of East Hutchinson residents had to be evacuated from their homes for months on end. The city dug wells all over Hutchinson to allow the gas to burn freely in hopes of relieving the pressure and avoiding future explosions. Thank God, it worked.

We had no idea that this devastating event would set the tone for the rest of the year. Within our church, tragedies began to take place that only heightened our anxiety and forever altered who we were. The first was the sudden death of a gentleman who had been instrumental in helping build our building. He had been helping a local charity renovate an old apartment complex when he fell down an elevator shaft. Unbelievable, right? Gut wrenching. Why did this happen?

Three weeks later, before we could begin processing his death, a car accident claimed the lives of four young teenagers from our youth group. Again, the pain was unbearable. Again, the community grieved with these families. Our teens were overwhelmed. What was going on? But it was just the beginning.

Then came that Tuesday in September. It was such a beautiful day that I rolled down my car window and breathed deeply. Every day had been filled with helping grieving people deal with tragic turns. I was fully aware that we were struggling to process this pain.

As I walked into my office, our receptionist was weeping. Without a word, she simply pointed to the TV that hung in our waiting room. Over and over again, the news broadcast replayed the images of the airplanes hitting each of the Twin Towers, blooms of flames and smoke engulfing the buildings.

I'm sure every one of us remembers where we were on September 11, 2001, when nineteen members of the Islamic extremist group al-Qaeda hijacked four commercial airliners and committed the deadliest terrorist attack on US soil. The attacks killed nearly three thousand people, injured six thousand more, and caused at least $10 billion in infrastructure and property damage.

Without question, 9/11 was the defining moment of the

twenty-first century for Americans. I will never forget going to the grocery store that evening—the silence was deafening. Everyone was stunned. In the midst of unexplainable death and loss, we all needed comfort, hope, and answers. The following Sunday, September 16, churches all over America overflowed with distraught visitors, and we were no exception. I encouraged our congregation that we "sorrow not as those who have no hope." We prayed and wept and reached out to Christ. Everyone felt unified by our common tragedy. We were all brothers and sisters, Americans united in grief.

As days and weeks went by, I could sense the stress building in the minds and hearts of my neighbors. We were all filled with multiple emotions at the same time—pain, grief, anger, and a deep nagging sense of something wrong with the world. Locally, nationally, and globally, life as we knew it seemed to be unraveling. Christians talked about the end of the world. And America was about to attack our enemy, if we could just figure out who he was and where he was hiding.

After 9/11, church attendance around the nation exploded overnight, but they didn't come to join a family—they came to be reassured, though there's nothing wrong with that. Many people discovered the innocence of our habitation with the Lord and flooded into the sanctuary in hopes of an experience of their own. Many of these folks simply wanted an escape from their fear—not a transforming relationship with the God of love and compassion. They didn't come to be a friend or to find the greatest Friend. They didn't come to do the deep work of finding themselves and following Christ. They came to consume, not to be consumed.

If you're an actor or an athlete, you want to be discovered.

But if you're a servant of the Lord, you would rather not be noticed. Today, I understand why the early Christians hid in the catacombs. Our individualistic, consumerist culture can crush the life out of you so quickly. No wonder Peter said, "Get out while you can; get out of this sick and stupid culture!" (Acts 2:40, MSG)

Unfortunately, the services became performances that met the appetite of our consumers. What had been magnificent became empty for those of us who had been there for a long time. What once gave energy now sucked life not only from me but from the original seekers. Fears and frustrations began to surface. Someone would say to me, "Pastor, the anointing was good today." I walked away wondering if that was code for "it wasn't last week."

I grew increasingly frustrated. Sunday after Sunday, I drove home disappointed with what was happening. What was so real, so pure, was being polluted by a culture that simply wanted another fix. Empty and confused, I began to cry out for that first love, now lost. I knew the power of the Lord was real—I'd seen miraculous things with my own eyes—but far too often we settle for false finish lines. We settle for having the presence of God in the house without remaining at his feet. We have a tendency to come and visit rather than staying with him.

By November, church attendance across the country had returned to its pre-9/11 numbers. According to George Barna, few of these people experienced anything sufficiently life-changing to capture their ongoing attention and allegiance. "They tended to appreciate the moments of comfort they received but were unaware of anything sufficiently unique or beneficial as to redesign their lifestyle to integrate a deeper level of spiritual involvement," he said.*

The tragedies in our community continued. My oldest son was engaged to be married that year. His fiancée had bought her dress, the venue was booked, the guest list complete. We were in full-on wedding planning mode when the phone rang with more bad news. On September 18, a week after the terrorist attack on the World Trade Center, my daughter-in-law's father was getting his hair cut when he slumped forward in the barber's chair. He never regained consciousness. At forty-six, he was gone, the victim of a brain aneurysm.

A month later, his close friend—the husband of one of my associate pastors—was killed when his car was broadsided. He was on his way to take one of his sons to school when another vehicle ran a stop sign. The accident left his wife and three young sons fatherless. These two tragedies rocked our faith.

Within a six-month period, eighteen people from my congregation had died. I found myself at a complete loss as to how to address our collective agony from the pulpit, and my interactions with my fellow pastors only furthered my confusion. The collective response was that there must be a lack of faith or undisclosed sin in someone's life. These statements added even greater pain to an already painful situation.

In 2002, a well-known television evangelist flew into Hutchinson on his private jet for a speaking engagement at our church. I picked him up at the airport, but halfway to the church, he said, "Oh, wait—we've got to go back. I left my jewelry in the airport bathroom."

---

* "How America's Faith Has Changed Since 9-11," Barna, November 26, 2001, https://www.barna.com/research/how-americas-faith-has-changed-since-9-11/

I took him back to the FBO, and when he returned to the car, he was wearing an extremely expensive diamond ring and bracelet worth much more that I could grasp. He dressed impeccably in the finest suits and ties. That evening at church, he walked the aisles, saying, "The anointing of money is on my life. All you've got to do is touch me."

I felt like a thousand light bulbs had just illuminated my perspective. I was raised in a church culture that thought the poorer you were, the holier you were. The concept of God's financial blessing was a breath of fresh air. But any teaching taken to the extreme is to the detriment of the teaching. Many believers began to think that if you weren't prosperous and healthy, then something must be wrong. This kind of teaching had no theology for suffering.

I remember the day one of the leading voices of the movement looked at me and said, "Quintin, do you have a plane yet?" When I said no, he said, "What's wrong with you? You need to expand your faith."

That philosophy of performance-based faith reminded me of the shame-based perspective I had grown up with. I drove home from that conversation thinking about the devastation my community had been experiencing for more than a year. Silently, undetected forces can gather beneath the surface of our lives. Like natural gas collecting in underground crevices, our lives can be injected with ideas and philosophies that ultimately cause damage. For the second time in my life, I realized that bad religious concepts can create a dangerous environment. It only takes a spark to ignite that invisible, unseen substance.

During the summer of 2002, I was sitting in my office when a young couple walked into the church, asking to speak with me.

They had moved to Hutchinson for work, and we had become their family away from home. They are some of my favorite people in the whole world. We loved them then and even more now. They were expecting their second child. As I hugged them, I knew something was very wrong.

"Something's not right with the baby," the momma-to-be said. Her tears flowed freely. "They can't find a heartbeat. We're headed to the hospital."

My own heart nearly stopped. They delivered a boy named Ian who was born with trisomy 18, a chromosomal disorder. He never took a breath. Once again, our hearts cried out, "Why?" The question overwhelmed us.

The day after we buried Ian, another couple in the church went into early labor. The baby only lived a few days. She too suffered from chromosomal defects. Within two short weeks, we had walked through the same hell with two different sets of parents.

Our country, our city, our congregation had suffered through a year of death and loss and constant questioning. Why? How? Had we any answers, I doubt they would have provided any comfort. We have all been raised to believe that life is supposed to make sense. We have all been taught to think before we do something and to have a reason for our actions. When we are faced with things outside of our control, it's normal to ask why things are happening. We go looking for reasons.

Our congregation was simply unprepared to deal with this level of suffering. Our faith was an inch deep and a mile wide. We hadn't made room for brokenness nor allowed space for suffering. Though it wasn't something we would have discussed openly, we viewed the common trials and tribulations of life as judgments of God or attacks from the enemy. Conspiracy theories abounded. Any vulnerability became a question about the maturity of a believer's faith.

While two different families grieved the deaths of their newborn babies, I overheard questions like, "Who sinned?" or even worse, "If only they'd had more faith." In the midst of losing close friends and children, we were struggling. Our local community, as well as the rest of the country, was trying to make sense of the circumstances of our era, and our faith was cracking under the weight of these challenges.

As we moved into the twenty-first century, something was shifting. The countercultural nature of the kingdom of God was getting lost. The weaknesses of the modern church were glaring in my face. The culture had lost its mind. Sirens were going off in my head. I could see red lights flashing in the rearview mirror. The message of God's unmerited favor had been mutated into financial prosperity and the authority to rule others.

We had allowed the way of the world to creep into our lives. If you did everything right, you could expect blessings and favor, but if not, you would be judged. Christians across America attested to such a notion. National religious leaders went so far as to declare on television that gays, feminists, abortionists, and the ACLU were to blame for 9/11.

In church, we simply sang louder and longer. We sang warfare songs with intensity. Surely, we would be the ones to turn the wrath of God away from our community. People were afraid they were sinning or too close to those who were. People began to criticize each other. Friends began to point out each other's weaknesses. Decades of partisan politics had creeped into our church, and divisions between segments of the congregation grew wider.

During this season, I began to realize that I needed a mentor. As I read the writings of the early church fathers, I realized that I needed a father of the faith. I went to several men I knew, and each time, I encountered the same answer: "Quintin, I don't know what to do." They didn't criticize my questions, my hunger, or my searching. Each of them acknowledged that I was asking good questions, but none of them had good answers.

Toward the end of the revival, I woke up one day and felt tarnished. My radical Christianity, my love for Lutheranism, my passion for the Holy Spirit had all been tainted by the consumeristic individualism of our modern culture. I'm a radical Jesus guy, but one day early in the new millennium, I realized I had cheered when troops dropped bombs in Desert Storm. I felt so ashamed—Jesus would never have thrown a party for war. I believed everything Jesus said, but I had also allowed myself to get caught up in the extreme faith movement and the cultural accommodation of that season. Something had gone very wrong. Somehow, I had lost my way.

Every time I prayed to the Lord for direction, I heard a voice in my soul say, "This is your responsibility. My people need to know more than they know. They need to know me more deeply." My congregation lacked spiritual depth—and it was entirely my fault. I took it very personally. I deeply love and appreciate all the people who have taken an interest in me over the years—I had found great success as part of their culture—but I came to recognize a fundamental weakness in our modern theology, one that had left me and my church ill equipped for harsh realities of our daily lives.

Sometimes life just happens, and for reasons we may never

understand. We are called to trust God in every situation. Trust GOD from the bottom of your heart; don't try to figure out everything on your own. Listen for GOD'S voice in everything you do, everywhere you go; he's the one who will keep you on track. (Proverbs 3:5-6, MSG) Trust is a hard thing for us, right? We want to have an explanation for everything. We need to have a formula for everything. We want guarantees, causes and effects. We want to perform so that we can acquire and control our world.

Somewhere along the journey, I had allowed the modern culture to pollute the ideals I had grown to love and cherish. It reminded me of the old story of how to cook a frog—you just put him in a pot of water and slowly turn up the heat until he's boiling. And like the climactic scene in *The Lion King*, I could hear Mufasa saying, "You have forgotten who you are, and so forgotten me. Look inside yourself, Simba—you are more than what you have become."

SEASON THREE

STIRRINGS

CHAPTER 10

Convergence

"Nothing is ever lost; things only become irretrievable. What is lost, then, it is the method of their retrieval and what we discover is not the thing itself, but the overgrown path, the secret staircase, the ancient sewer."

—François Aussermain

One day, I was commiserating with an Orthodox friend about how we were a mile wide and an inch deep in understanding who God was and how he interacts in our lives. In a culture of consumerism, we had settled for far too little. We wanted simple answers to complicated questions. I was searching for something deeper, or at least something that made more sense.

He handed me several things to read, including *The Orthodox Way* by Kallistos Ware, *Dark Night of the Soul* by St. John of the Cross, and works by St. Ignatius of Loyola, the martyr Polycarp,

St. John of Patmos, and Teresa of Ávila. I had read classic writings in the past and found an affinity for them, but he assured me there was so much more to God and to his church than I had ever allowed myself to be exposed to.

Among the ancient writings, I saw how these men and women from the church's earliest years were martyred for their faith. God hadn't stopped their suffering either. I was discovering a church much older and much larger than I had ever imagined. But like the Ethiopian reading Isaiah in Acts 8, I needed someone like Philip to explain to me what I was reading. I was not expecting Philip to look like Mike Warnke.

I had first heard of Mike, a Christian comic, back in the early 1970s at the height of the Jesus movement. They were a bunch of long-haired Jesus freaks who took the Sermon on the Mount seriously as a call to be countercultural. Mike was one of the great voices of that movement. He was also the perfect friend for me because I knew he was never content with the status quo.

In the early 1980s, I listened to Mike's cassette tapes constantly. One evening I was driving across Tennessee from Chattanooga to Memphis—a long drive—with three other men who worked for my dad. After listening to "Hey Doc," one of my favorite Mike Warnke stories, the two guys asked me how they could know Christ. I stopped the car, and we all got out alongside the road. I had them kneel down, and I simply led them in a prayer of repentance, the only thing I knew to do. I later baptized them in a hotel swimming pool.

Another ten years passed before I met Mike in person. Annie and I were attending a Kenneth Copeland conference at Eagle Mountain International Church in Newark, Texas, when Mike walked up to the table where Annie and I were seated.

Annie nearly shouted, "You're Mike Warnke!"

His reply was typical: "Yeah, I have been for a long time."

Since then, Mike and I have grown to be great friends. Over the years, he has encouraged me in my journey of embracing the Eucharist in our worship and in our pursuit of blending every aspect of Christian worship into our services. Every time he came and preached for me during those years, I expressed my concerns about the shallowness of our faith in the face of suffering. I also shared that I was struggling to understand how we fit into the larger Christian tradition, but I felt the need to embrace our deeper Christian heritage. I knew that any critic of the church was dangerous because you cannot separate Christ from his church. I saw great weaknesses in our current expression of church, but at the same time, I knew we were his church. I'm so thankful that in the midst of my seeking a better understanding, God sent a friend.

"Quintin, I have some friends I'd like you to meet," he said. Once again, God was leading me to a friend of a friend.

He introduced me to Wayne Boosahda, then-presiding bishop of the Communion of Evangelical Episcopal Churches (CEEC). The CEEC was one of several communions emerging from the convergence movement, which brought together the three principal streams of Christian worship—sacramental, evangelical, and charismatic. The sacraments include the Eucharist, baptism, liturgy from the Book of Common Prayer, ancient rites and rituals, as well as the historic episcopacy and continuity with the ancient church. The evangelical expression encompasses the authority and centrality of the scriptures, teaching and preaching, and salvation by faith in the death and resurrection of Jesus Christ. The charismatic stream highlights the work and infilling of the Holy Spirit through praise and gifts like prophecy, healing, or speaking in tongues. The three living streams are a trinity of worship reflecting, respectively, the Father, the Son, and the Holy Spirit.

From my new friends, I learned that the history of the convergence movement dated back to the 1950s and the writings of Lesslie Newbigin, a British theologian and missionary to India. A prolific author, Newbigin wrote in *The Household of God* that the church was constituted of the "Protestant, Catholic, and Pentecostal."* These three facets were, in his opinion, the "starting point for reunification efforts within the church."†

The 1960s saw the emergence of the charismatic movement, in which liturgical and mainline churches around the world experienced an outpouring of the Holy Spirit. The 1967 Catholic Charismatic Renewal at Duquesne University in Pittsburg, Pennsylvania, then lit a fire to the ecumenism between Catholics and Pentecostals. While Catholics were being baptized in the Holy Spirit, evangelicals were beginning to recognize the importance of historic Christianity, a gap caused by the much needed Reformation that began in 1517.

Dr. Robert E. Webber, a longtime professor at Wheaton College and the founder of the Institute for Worship Studies in Jacksonville, Florida, studied the early church and examined

---

* Lesslie Newbigin. *The Household of God: Lectures on the Nature of the Church* (London: SCM Press, 1953), ix.

† Rt. Rev. Ryan Mackey, "Three Streams and One River: The History and Future of the Convergence Movement," The Communion of Evangelical Episcopal Churches, https://static1.squarespace.com/static/581e24b06a49638d950ca1fe/t/5b68ba010e2e729ed65bef47/1533590019156/RMPaper.pdf.

his own evangelical context. In the introduction of *Common Roots,* Webber wrote, "The major issue facing evangelical Christianity, the one from which all other problems flow, is a kind of evangelical amnesia. Evangelicals have forgotten the past. There is a need to change . . . our 'sadly deficient' state of historical knowledge."*

In the late 1980s and early 1990s, Michael and Beth Owen, Wayne Boosahda, and Robert Wise began engaging in conversations around the concept of convergence, especially as it related to the celebration of the Eucharist in the ancient church and their desire to see this restored in their experience of the contemporary church.

The men and women on this journey found themselves drawn to a renewed commitment to the sacramental life, the table of the Lord in particular. They also began to rethink and examine their understanding and practice of the Christian faith in light of the early church. The more they prayed, studied, and reflected on what they were learning, the deeper grew their hunger and desire to embrace the whole church, not simply one stream of it. They began to see the church as truly one body, and the different streams of the church brought needed gifts, treasures, and elements to the whole. The founders of the convergence movement desired not only to see the church as one but to embrace brothers and sisters in streams of the church with which they were less familiar so they could learn from them. They also felt they were being called to work for the greater unity of the church.

In 1992, Boosahda wrote a definitive article on the

---

* Robert E. Webber, *Common Roots* (Grand Rapids: Zondervan, 1978), 15.

convergence movement for Robert Webber's publication, *The Complete Library of Christian Worship*. That paper was a touch point for several other folks who were exploring the confluence of these three streams of Christian expression. The highest value of the convergence movement is the unity of the church by bringing together the various expressions of the body of Christ.

A number of other theologians began to have an impact on the imagination of the evangelical and charismatic branches of the church. Among them was Father Peter Gillquist, who grew up Lutheran and was involved with Campus Crusade for Christ before ultimately becoming an archpriest in the Antiochian Orthodox Church. Dr. Tom Oden, an influential Methodist theologian and author, tirelessly wrote, lectured, and encouraged Christians to return to what he called "classical Christianity" and encouraged believers to rely on the wisdom of the early church. Dr. Thomas Howard, a highly acclaimed writer and scholar and brother of former missionary Elisabeth Elliot, became an Episcopalian in his mid-twenties and later joined the Catholic Church. Dr. Bob Stamps was a Methodist pastor and university chaplain whose post-graduate studies focused on the Eucharist. He brought many evangelicals into a rich sacramental and liturgical experience. The Reverend Dr. Donald Lacy, a Methodist pastor, built bridges between Protestants and Roman Catholics and wrote extensively on finding reasons to celebrate the Virgin Mary.

In 1993, these leaders attended a conference called 'Treasures Old and New, Convergence Renewal in the Contemporary and Ancient Churches," held in Oklahoma City, Oklahoma. The conference was co-hosted by Michael and Beth Owen's church and Wayne Boosahda's ministry, The Fellowship of St. Barnabas the Encourager. More than 130 Christian leaders were present, including many who became leaders of the convergence movement across the country. Attendees included Protestant, Catholic, and Orthodox Christians.

In October of 1995, three hundred people gathered in Fredericksburg, Virginia, where the first two bishops of the CEEC were consecrated, and twenty-five pastors and seven deacons were also ordained. Twenty-five congregations from various denominations joined the new Communion. The CEEC is centered in Anglican spirituality and worship but isn't formally affiliated with the Anglican Church overseen by the archbishop of Canterbury. Today, the CEEC has a footprint in twenty-two countries on six continents, and we continue to grow daily.

Interestingly enough, I had first witnessed the signs of convergence in Cuba back in 1991. Every church I visited, whether Methodist, Baptist, Catholic, or Pentecostal, understood the value of cultivating a friendship with not only Christ but also with every fellow believer. There was no distinction between the churches. In each one, I witnessed the same expressions—the scriptures, some form of sacrament, and the Holy Spirit. These Cuban brothers and sisters were living and worshipping as one people, as friends. It was an amazing experience. In many ways, God was seeding convergence in my heart.

By the time I met Wayne Boosahda, I was forty-seven years old, and despite the success I'd had as a Word of Faith minister, I needed a mentor, a father in the faith. Up to that point, I didn't know how to articulate what I thought God was doing in our fellowship. I have often said that Bishop Wayne gave me language for what I was feeling and thinking. I realized I was convergence before I was convergence. For twenty years, I thought I was quietly, even oddly, blending my Nazarene, Pentecostal, Lutheran, and charismatic encounters into something that seemed to work in our out-of-the-way, rather unique little church. I didn't have any real way of explaining it to anyone. Most of the time, I feared I was doing something wrong.

Reconnecting to church continuity helped answer my dilemma on a theology of suffering. The church during its first three centuries, pre-Constantine, was the clearest expression of the church. The martyrs of that era certainly didn't die for lack of faith but for the gospel of Christ. Our spiritual journeys will always be shrouded in seasons of suffering that can't be explained. Everyone is certain they know everything—no mystery, no shades of gray. Certitude is the death of faith in the twenty-first century. The theology and spiritual insights of the ancient church help recover that uncertainty.

The ideals of convergence resonated with my soul. These friends opened my ears to hear the sound of rushing waters as the great streams of the church converged into one mighty river. I could hear the sound of different expressions of the church coming together in the unity of faith. My imagination was released from the limitations of denominationalism, cultural accommodation, and political partisanship.

I now had language to communicate that our churches were involved in something far greater than our own lives or even our own generations. We are joined to God by his grace, not simply so that we can go to heaven, but that we might be restored into relationship with him and with one another. We are brought into a friendship, a union with God, that is manifested in the communion of the church. This is a mystery beyond description that includes so many more souls than we have ever imagined.

The convergence movement called me into a conversation I didn't even know was taking place—a conversation that leads to communion. The church is so much more than an institution, a missions organization, or a franchise with a targeted audience. The church is more than a well-managed human organization with a common set of goals. The church fathers taught that the church is the continuation of the ministry of Jesus. I would suggest that the church is a Spirit-created, Spirit-led community of redeemed people who possess the power of God's presence. The church is the social manifestation of a spiritual reality and is intended to be a safe, sacred hiding place where people can find forgiveness, healing, meaning, and friendship.

One of the many reasons my heart has so resonated with the convergence movement and its passion for unity is that I have witnessed firsthand the pain and confusion caused by division within the church. Over the past fifteen years, I've had numerous conversations with residents of my local community who have shared how they've been hurt and turned off by their experiences in our churches.

The common denominator comes to rest on our hypocrisy—the incongruence between what we say we believe and how we live—as well as the division among us—our doctrinal differences and the judgments we make against people who believe or worship in another manner.

I can still see the faces of one young couple who met me in my office. "We went to four different churches when we were first married," said the young husband, "and we heard four completely different things. One of them said that if we weren't baptized in their church, we wouldn't go to heaven. Another told us that all Catholics were going to hell. We went into one in the middle of a church split. We don't mean to be disrespectful, but which one is right? Really, pastor, if you guys don't have it together and live that love thing, how are we supposed to know what to think?"

They were genuinely searching for answers. And this was not an isolated incident.

From another young man I met in a local restaurant, I heard: "You church people are all alike—you talk about loving people, but you don't even get along. The Baptists don't like the Catholics, and the Pentecostals think they're better than everyone. And what about those dudes on TV always asking for money? At least the Buddhists get along with each other."

He was so matter-of-fact. I was trying to capture his spiritual attention and talk to him about faith and being involved with the church. I tried to salvage the conversation. "It's true we're not a perfect group of people, but we're forgiven."

"Ah, man don't give me that old line. I don't think you guys even know your own story. Either you all came from the same place or not. Either the forgiveness stuff is real or it's not. If that Jesus guy really did exist, then you would all be part of the same gang. You would all run together. At least my guys hang together."

He didn't even blink, just stared me straight in the eye, almost daring me to continue the debate. "My mom and dad went to church when I was a kid," he continued. "Yeah, they got a divorce. That was hard. And you know what? Our church treated Mom and Dad as if they had the plague or something.

Nobody even tried to help them. They just kept talking about sin and stuff like that. Church? I don't need it. Now leave me alone."

These kinds of conversations have repeated over and over again. The topics are vast: divorce and remarriage, clothing and tattoos, alcohol, women in ministry. We will debate everything—who's in, who's out, who can we associate with or not. The seeds of confusion come not only from the pews or outside the church but from leadership as well.

A reverend of another denomination once told me, "I will not have those people participate in this event. We are evangelicals—they are not. In fact, I'm not sure those Catholics or Episcopalians are even saved."

"Oh, come now," I responded. "Surely we can agree to get along for one evening?"

"No, I don't think so. My people would never stand for it. We aren't allowed to be with people who don't believe what we believe. It's just not permitted."

I stuttered to find words. "Don't you think that they are part of God's family? I mean, they believe that Jesus is the son of God who died and rose for them. They trust in God's mercy, just like we do."

"I don't know that or not, but I know they aren't one of us."

And with that, he turned and walked away. Those words still ring in my ears: "They aren't one of us."

That conversation was such a contrast to the prayer that Jesus prayed before his death. The convergence movement centers around what Jesus says in John 17:20-21: "I do not pray for these alone, but also for those who will believe in Me through their word; that they all may be one, as You, Father, are in Me, and I in You; that they also may be one in Us, that the world may believe that You sent Me." He makes it sound like our perfection, our completeness, our wholeness, and our healing are all related to being in a unique, intimate relationship—a friendship that he describes as being "one" with one another.

These conversations have fueled my concern over the lack of unity in the body of Christ. We have allowed our differences to separate us from one another. And we have constructed "communities" around all sorts of things other than God's presence. We are so splintered and fragmented that many of those who once participated in the church have simply given up trying to figure it all out. If I believe the prayer of John 17—that our oneness affects the world's ability to believe—then I must assume that the lack of unity hinders the world's capacity to know Christ. Jesus indicated that our intimate friendship with him and others is the witness the world needs and the very will of God. He didn't pray that we would write down some set of doctrines to follow or set up a church government to protect ourselves. He prayed not for the perfection of our doctrine but for the perfection of our ability to love one another and live in relationship. His prayer was simple and to the point: "Be one."

Unity will never be founded on doctrine or on a particular institution; unity will only flourish when we cherish and value the relationship between us more than we do our preferences. The essence of unity is true relationship.

The divisive culture of the church has become more and more apparent. Here in America, it's much like standing in Walmart (after you've made the decision to bypass Target, Sam's, and Costco) trying to decide which one of seventy-three types of laundry detergent to purchase. The church's descent into a market-driven corporation has left many wondering who or what constitutes an authentic expression of Christianity. What is real?

What does a follower of Christ look like? What do all Christ followers share in common with each other? What are the essentials of our faith? What does a holy man look like? Does he wear white and ride in the popemobile? Does he fly into town on a jet and wear expensive suits? Does he live on a farm and refuse to buy a car or have electricity in his home? Does he live in the towers of academia and argue over the interpretation of the scriptures? Is he Protestant, Roman Catholic, Orthodox, or Pentecostal? Is he onstage or just onscreen? Can he be a she? It is all so confusing!

For centuries, ecumenical movements have attempted to solve our theological, philosophical, and ecclesiastical differences through studies and summits. We have made great progress through those conversations, but any accomplishments have had little to no effect on local congregations in America. Why? Because the debates and discussions simply aren't clear and concise enough to make any difference in people's daily lives.

There is a sacred space where healing and wholeness can be found. An atmosphere where people can be restored to God's original intent. "By this everyone will know that you are my disciples, if you love one another." (John 13:35, NIV) God knows that our kindness and love for one another will have a far greater impact on the societies in which we live than our institutional accomplishments or our individual achievements.

This vision of unity is what I hope draws others into the convergence movement, whether they find themselves in a CEEC church or not. Our Communion doesn't own the convergence movement any more than a particular Pentecostal denomination owns the charismatic movement. Churches that embody the values of the convergence movement can create that sacred space for the healing of everyone who enters and ultimately for the healing of the world.

CHAPTER 11

Diocese of Restoration

"There is a river whose streams shall make glad the city of God."

—Psalm 46:4

In his book *Ancient-Future Faith*, Robert Webber wrote, "The goal of the church is to be a divine standard, a sign of God's incarnational presence and activity in history. In a postmodern world the most effective witness to a world of disconnected people is the church that forms community and embodies the reality of a new society. People in a postmodern world are not persuaded to faith by reason as much as they are moved to faith by participation in God's earthly community."*

I read those words over and over again. I was becoming

* Robert Webber, *Ancient-Future Faith: Rethinking Evangelicalism for a Postmodern World* (Grand Rapids: Baker Academic, 1999), 79.

painfully and yet joyfully aware that I was being given the opportunity to be part of a movement to live out a fuller and deeper understanding of the church. There was no turning back. I clearly remember the Lord speaking to me one evening about settling for a "pool party rather than the roaring rapids of a moving river." Like the man sitting at the edge of the pool waiting on an angel to stir the water in John 5, many people have settled for an occasional revival. The truth is that we are called to live in the midst of a moving river.

The prophet Ezekiel spoke of a river that flows out from the temple. A river that cannot be measured or crossed. A river that brings life and healing to all that is planted near it. "And it shall be that every living thing that moves, wherever the rivers go, will live. There will be a very great multitude of fish, because these waters go there; for they will be healed, and everything will live wherever the river goes." (Ezekiel 47:9)

I could no longer settle for occasional pool parties when I could hear the call of the river intended to flow out of the church, the body of Christ, the temple of God. A river that is the convergence of all of the streams of God.

I had pastored The Father's House for seventeen years. At the time, we had six other churches in the Father's House network of churches. In Latin America, we had more than fifty churches in our network. I was relating to churches all around the world. I considered the words of Jeremiah: "Stand at the crossroads and look; ask for the ancient paths, ask where the good way is, and walk in it, and you will find rest for your souls. But you said, 'We will not walk in it.'" (Jeremiah 6:16, NIV)

I had often wondered or second-guessed myself, playing and replaying my decision over and over in my head. But then one beautiful afternoon, the greatest theologian I know helped me see clearly.

I was pushing my granddaughter Avery Quinn, who was four years old at the time, on a swing set outside our home. I encouraged her to lean back and kick forward so that I didn't have to keep pushing her. She squealed with delight as she slowly got the hang of it. I'll never forget what she said: "Papa, look—if I lean way back and kick way forward I can go really high." In that moment, my heart was settled.

In 2002, I called our church leaders together to explain that I had to continue down this path of convergence. Contrary to what some thought, I never looked at this choice as though I was leaving anything but rather opening my heart to more of God and his church. I shared with my church council my desire to join the CEEC.

"I need to continue this journey—I need to walk this out," I said. "I'll resign if you want me to."

"No, pastor," they responded. "Where you go, we go."

In January of 2003, in a beautiful little church in Sparta, Tennessee, I was ordained as a presbyter in apostolic succession. I will never forget that service. As I lay on the floor of the sanctuary, I heard the Lord say, "Your journey is just beginning."

The first apostles received the faith "once and for all." (Jude 3:3) That faith has been passed forward from one generation to another, not simply through institutions or individuals. Just as we don't get to make faith up, we don't get to reshape the church based on the culture of our times. The unity of the church is hidden by the division that exists within the ranks of leadership. I wonder if one of the keys to recovering our unity might be found in the shared value of ordination.

That afternoon in Sparta, I began a journey of realizing the unity of both the old and new, the ancient and the future, the historical and the prophetic. "Then He said to them, 'Therefore every scribe instructed concerning the kingdom of heaven is like a householder who brings out of his treasure things new and old.'" (Matthew 13:52)

Never in my wildest dreams would I have imagined going on to serve as a bishop, a word missing from my vocabulary. Though I had planted a number of congregations, I had never given any consideration as to what that might mean. While working on my master's degree, I read about C. Peter Wagner's New Apostolic Reformation, a movement that advocated for the restoration of ancient offices of church governance, namely the prophet and apostle. As Wagner has stated, no one can appoint themselves an apostle—they are commissioned by their peers.* Wagner's writings were about as close as I had ever come to the word apostle or bishop. The idea didn't resonate with me, but it did stir me toward reading more about the apostolic office of a bishop, an older version of the apostolic tradition.

An ancient teaching of the church often attributed to Saint Ignatius of Antioch says, "Wherever the bishop shall appear, there let the multitude of the people also be; even as, wherever Jesus Christ is, there is the Catholic [universal or whole] Church."† Many throughout the history of the Christian Church have taken this to mean that each consecrated bishop gathers around themselves an expression of the body of Christ, namely

---

* C. Peter Wagner, "The New Apostolic Reformation Is Not a Cult," *Charisma News*, August 24, 2011.

† *Letter to the Smyrnaeans*, 8:2

a local church. Historically, a local church was a small grouping of a single parish in a city and its missions on the outskirts of the city and surrounding area. Each local church had an overseer, which some have understood to be a bishop, who was responsible for pastoring this local flock. Deacons assisted the bishop, and in some cases as determined by size and need, presbyters. Many local churches existed throughout the universal (catholic) church, each united under a local bishop just as the whole church was united under the headship of Jesus Christ.

CEEC leadership said, "Quintin, given that you're already leading multiple churches, you're already serving as a bishop."

As a bishop, I would continue overseeing our association of churches, which we renamed the Diocese of Restoration—I had long been a fan of Saint Francis and his pursuit of restoring the house of God. As I look back, I'm in awe of God's prophetic leading. I remain dedicated to restoring the ancient truths of the church, and I continue to focus on restoring every person to his or her identity in Christ.

My consecration took place on St. Patrick's Day, March 17, 2004. Fourteen current and retired CEEC bishops came to Hutchinson. Many of them had come from evangelical and Pentecostal contexts into a wider appreciation for the historical church. Others had come from Roman Catholic or Anglican churches who were discovering the power and presence of the Holy Spirit. All of us were committed to seeing the blending of everything the Lord has for us in our local churches.

That Wednesday afternoon, liturgical banners hung in front of the church, and along the altar, candles glowed in their wood and brass holders. Around the room were all of the symbols of the ancient church, and yet the worship was fully contemporary.

The room was charged with anticipation. Other ministers from town came to observe my consecration. The floor was packed, and overflow had gathered in the balcony. I stood in the foyer scared to death—I knew I was pushing every fundamentalist button possible.

The bishops and I processed down the aisle in full vestments. I wore vestments handmade by Annie and my mother-in-law, which was such an honor. We carried the cross and candles and a grand Bible. At the front, we each bowed and addressed the Eucharist table before setting down the staffs and miters. Then, the praise band broke into song and began playing the best charismatic worship music in the region. I love charismatic music, and I found myself dancing across the sanctuary dressed in full bishop's robes.

After three songs, we started the liturgy of consecration from the Book of Common Prayer. At one point, I lay prostrate on the floor, covered with a pall, and at another, the fourteen bishops laid hands on me to impart the gift of apostolic succession. The two-hour service was fully liturgical and fully Spirit-filled, a true convergent experience. We were celebrating the ancient, calling forth the future, and experiencing a change in the present.

Daniel Williams—the missionary to Europe I'd so admired who also planted Redeemer Church in Ponte Vedra Beach, Florida, in 1992—had since become a bishop in the CEEC as well. The evening of my consecration was the first time I met him in person, and the Lord knit our hearts together in a profound and eternal way. One of his greatest contributions to the convergence movement was his book, *The Sound of Rushing Waters*, in which he wrote, "The convergence movement is not an abandonment of any of the historical streams but a converging of each into a blended, contemporary expression. It is not so much a reaction to anything as a journey toward something. Perhaps we are in the midst of a new 'reformation' that will prepare us for the end-time harvest."*

Our congregation had celebrated the Eucharist every week for years. We had incorporated many different aspects of liturgy and the meanings of ancient time, including Advent, Lent, and Easter, into our worship. We used a few stoles and robes from time to time, particularly on high holy days. I thought I had prepared our church for the pageantry of the consecration.

But that night, the formality was a bit too much for some. A number of folks didn't like the idea of convergence. They struggled with the concepts of unity and embracing a history older than their denominational memory. The next several months were difficult—I felt like I was defending the faith of the last two thousand years.

I now realize that an attempt at unity challenges the identity of the separated expressions of the church. Most Christians identify themselves more with a tribe than they do with the Christ. Many are more connected with the founder of their denomination than with the Christ. Any real call for the unity of the whole will be opposed by tribalism—it's just human nature.

Convergence has a unique charism, a calling that allows us to engage and incorporate the ancient historical roots of the church in the midst of our evangelical and Pentecostal lives. We are attempting to live out of the fullness of our spirituality in our local churches and perhaps serve as a way forward in our

---

* Daniel W. Williams, *The Sound of Rushing Waters: A prophetic call to embrace the Great Commandment in order to fulfill the Great Commission* (Nashville: ACW Press, 2005), 16.

ecumenical calling. We truly want to be unifying—unlabeled and unaffected by denominational splits and spitting contests. We consider ourselves historically faithful, humbly charismatic, and truly contemplative, by which we mean bringing together scriptures, creeds, prayer, the work of the Holy Spirit, and spiritual formation in a way that transforms lives. All of us in the convergence movement have had that pull toward what we believe to be a more unified and authentic expression of the church.

We long to see the division of the church overcome by the prayer of Jesus found in John 17, "that they be one." We're not trying to build another institution that functions from the top down. We want instead to be a bridge that leans into something larger than ourselves. We also believe context matters. A CEEC church in India will look and operate differently from, say, one in New York.

As Rev. Cannon Rick E. Hatfield wrote, "Emphasizing the interweaving of Spirit, scripture, and sacrament, we identify and stand in connection with the ancient way of following Jesus Christ . . . as well as with many of the values and practices of Celtic Christianity. . . . We consider ourselves as friends and family on a common journey and quest of spiritual discovery rooted in the ancient faith. . . . We are excited pioneers and explorers of spiritual treasures old and new encountered through relationship with our living Lord, one another, and his people throughout history.*

* Rev. Cannon Rick E. Hatfield, *Apostolic Succession in the Convergence Movement* (Jacksonville: Logos College Publishing, 1996), 161.

⁂

One afternoon in 2006, we had gathered for a series of meetings at Redeemer Church near Jacksonville when life came full circle, a moment I'll never forget. I was sitting in a conference room when in walked Tony Palmer—my former Word of Faith associate from South Africa. I hadn't seen him in years, but now here we were, two friends who had found each other again.

"How in the world did you get here?" I asked.

"How in the world did *you* get here?" he retorted, laughing.

Unbeknownst to either of us, we had both found our way into the convergence movement.

On trips back to Italy to visit Emiliana's family, who were Roman Catholic, Tony had encountered the Catholic Charismatic Renewal, a movement within the Catholic Church that absorbed the Pentecostal and evangelical traditions of praise and worship, healing, and an expectation of spiritual gifts. Through the charismatics, Emiliana returned to the Catholic Church, and Tony and his young children accompanied her to Sunday Mass.

In 2003, they moved to Italy to work with Matteo Calisi, head of the Catholic Charismatic Renewal in Italy. Tony increasingly felt at home in the Catholic Church but was unable to affiliate, so he formed an ecumenical group the Ark Community. In 2004, Tony met Bishop Robert Wise, one of the founders of the CEEC who had been teaching at Catholic Fraternity gatherings. We had both found our home in the CEEC.

From the moment we reconnected, Tony and I shared a glorious relationship fueled by our vision for the CEEC and for unity in the body of Christ. Just as God had reconnected Tony and me, the Lord would soon bring someone else into our lives who shared our dream of unity in the church, someone who would also call me friend.

CHAPTER 12

Betrayal

> "Isn't interesting that Jesus's circle of friends included Judas?"
>
> —Tommy Barnett

Late one afternoon in December of 2008, I was staring out my office window, watching the shadows grow longer. A cold and windy day, a few flakes of snow blew along the sidewalk outside, reminding me of the day we buried my dad. I shuddered at the memory. I was trying to settle my thoughts.

A guest speaker was flying into town that night, and beginning the next day, we would have a busy schedule. Why I agreed to do this just three weeks before Christmas, I'll never understand. Our staff was stressed—I'd said yes to his request without thinking. But he's my friend, and he said he simply felt like the Lord had told him to come. According to the staff, I just hadn't thought it through very well.

The loud ring of my cell phone startled me out of my ruminations. The ring tone belonged to someone more familiar to me—my daughter, Heather. She had been in the morning staff meeting, but I hadn't seen her since lunch.

"What's up, honey?" I asked. "Where ya been?"

Silence.

"Are you there?" Maybe I had weak cell-phone service. I moved around my desk to see if I could get a better signal. "Can you hear me?"

I could hear her breathing hard, gasping. It's a sound I'll never forget—I was instantly jolted. Adrenaline surged through my body. "Are you all right? Where are you?"

"I'm so sorry!" she said, her sobs loud and uncontrollable. "Daddy, I'm so sorry."

"Where are you? Talk to me!" Now I was sobbing, too. My beautiful, amazing child was in trouble, and I didn't know what had happened.

Heather's entire life revolved around our church. She had been involved in all aspects of our ministry—worship music, youth group, children's ministry. I counted on her for many things. For the last several years, she had managed our child-care center. She hadn't dated much, saying she wasn't ready, and we never pushed the issue. She simply went to school, worked with us, and lived in the apartment over our garage.

But now I didn't know where she was. I screamed for my wife, Annie, who was sitting in the adjacent office. I lowered my voice, trying to remain calm. "Heather, honey, just tell me where you are."

"Just outside your door, Daddy. I'm sitting here in my car."

I don't remember racing to her car, but the next memory is of her falling into my arms. I practically carried her back into the church and into my office where her mother waited, her face filled with panic. We collapsed onto the couch, and her mom started checking every inch of Heather's body.

"Blood," Annie said. "Quintin, there's blood."

A stream of thick red oozed from Heather's left upper arm. Annie helped her remove her sweater to reveal a puncture wound.

"I'm okay," said Heather. "It's not as bad as it looks."

Annie ordered me to get a wet towel. She applied pressure until she was satisfied the wound was no longer gushing. My daughter, bleeding and weeping, sat on the couch, utterly distraught.

"I've ruined everything, Daddy. Don't be angry with me. I should have told you years ago. I just didn't know how."

She convulsed into another series of sobs. Her mom was holding her now, rocking her like a baby.

I sat in front of her on the floor. "Whatever it is, it's going to be okay. Mom and I love you. We'll figure it out. All that matters is that you're okay."

My mind swirled like the snowflakes outside. What was going on? Who had done this? *Years ago*, she said. Years of what?

"It's my fault. I made him mad. I shouldn't have said anything. I know better. If I'd just kept my mouth shut. Don't be mad, Dad. I'm so sorry."

Tears were rolling down my wife's pained face, falling onto her sweater. We were numb, paralyzed by the moment. Neither of us understood what Heather was saying.

Slow and steady, I asked, "Who did this to you, baby?"

When Heather named one of our associate pastors—a close friend, a fellow minister—I felt a blade pierce me to the core of my being. The blood drained from my face. My head spun. I thought I might be sick. I glanced at my wife to see her face reflecting the same horror.

A tsunami of questions poured from my mouth. "I don't understand. Why would he do this? Where were you? What was going on?"

Heather slowly caught her breath and began stuttering through her sobs. "He's been angry with me for years. You know how he is. If only I could just stay quiet and avoid him and not make him mad. It's all my fault."

It was true that the tension between them was constant. I had just chalked it up to her age and his lack of patience with someone eighteen years younger. Something much more sinister had been going on. I wanted this whole scenario to be a dream, but the nightmare was real. The wind howled, and the cold crawled across the floor—no walls, no protection from the elements. No more hiding, no more secrets—ready or not, here comes the truth. I couldn't control my tears. I've spent my whole life speaking and consoling, but I had nothing—the silence was deafening.

"Dad, I can't take it anymore! I'm so tired of being hurt. I'm so sorry, I thought I could handle it, but I can't. Don't hate me! Please forgive me."

"Oh, baby, no, no, no!" I said. "We love you—it's okay. Stop, stop, stop!"

Tears, dried blood, our beautiful, strong, confident daughter reduced to this scared little girl. What happened? Our minds darted from one bad scene to another. Our imaginations ran rampant. Embraced from both sides now, Heather stumbled on, testing the grace we had to give this perpetrator.

"I promised him I would never tell," she said through sobs. The fear in her eyes was so real, the panic in her voice deafening. "I'm scared! Dad, I'm so sorry. I just can't take it anymore. Oh, God, what have I done?"

She was a beautiful baby. I bought her a pink fluffy dress to bring her home from the hospital. She had always been the happiest child. She was so adorable. She really was that cute little girl that every daddy is proud to have. That cold December night, I became Dad. Just Dad, not pastor, not bishop. A father was being born anew, right there with the cold wind pressing in and around our lives. I became what I was called to be, Dad, and nothing more. All that mattered was my family and my community.

It would take days for the details to unfold until I felt I would never find the bottom of the abyss. Detail after detail plunged us further into the darkness of despair. Years of abuse. We knew it had to be years because of the incoherent statements she was making. She refused to answer when we asked, "When did this start?" She kept giving us percentages instead, the amount for which she felt responsible. Over the next several months of intensive counseling, we would learn that abuse victims often struggle with shame and guilt, believing they somehow chose or deserved what had happened to them.

We would later learn that it started when my little girl was only twelve. Twelve! Innocent, with her curly hair and constant giggles. Beanie babies and slumber parties. How did we miss this? Years of sexual and physical abuse. He was like a brother to me. What the hell? I trusted him with my family, my life, the church. I cried constantly.

The tale was told, at least for now. Something took over,

something I can't quite describe. I knew I needed to tell someone what had happened. I couldn't be trusted to make clear-headed decisions. I knew in that moment that I couldn't handle this by myself. I picked up the phone and called my best friend. I never called during office hours because I knew he was seeing patients.

"Yes, I need you to interrupt him," I told his receptionist. "It's an emergency. I'll wait." I heard my own voice, detached and distant, as if emanating from another person.

The instant I heard Terry's voice, something shifted in me. I told him no one was dying, but it couldn't wait. "I need you now. We'll go home and wait for you there."

Darkness had descended by the time we walked outside to the car. My tears never ceased, nor the stabs of pain rising in my heart. Shadows of lies had hidden the hideous reality of abuse. Walls were coming down, brick by brick, the pounding relentless. Heather moved from thought to thought as if remembering a dream, each revelation raising more and more questions for her mother and me.

Annie and I were sitting in our living room on either side of Heather when Terry arrived. The transition had only taken twenty minutes, but years of secrets had been laid bare. Anger boiled within me, but I couldn't go there just yet. No words can describe the flood of emotions raging in my soul.

Heather started her story again, this time speaking more calmly and succinctly. The story was clear, and our pain was unbearable. We cried and cried and cried. He held us all and prayed. I now realize the irony of one friend's betrayal and the healing love of another. If Terry hadn't been there, we could never have taken those first few steps. In moments of both joy and pain, we always reach for those we know we can trust and with whom we can be transparent. Friends are our only hope. In those moments when you think you are alone, God is always present. He is present in the friendships forged by the challenges of life.

Terry turned to me. “I’ve got this, Quintin. Trust me, okay?”

I remembered the first time he said that to me. Trust—it sounds easy, but it takes everything you have to trust. In the midst of broken trust, the Lord will ask you to continue to trust.

He called the abuser and told him we needed to talk. Not long afterward, the doorbell rang. Ninety minutes after the start of this ordeal, I was staring down the man who had sexually abused my daughter. I still can’t believe he got in his car and drove to my house. I realize now that he probably thought he would lie his way through the whole situation.

I finally blurted out, “Is this true? Did you do this?”

I’m not sure what I expected him to say, but I wasn’t ready for what I heard.

“Yes, I did.”

I still have trouble processing the calm, matter-of-fact way in which he replied. I no longer recognized this brother of mine. I felt I wasn’t even in the room but watching us all from a great distance, even as I heard my wife breathing and Heather weeping. The wind outside blew even stronger, and yet the air was still and absurdly quiet, as if nothing was moving. Time had stopped.

I listened to my own voice, yet it wasn’t me, say, “Well, I guess we will see if I can live what I believe.”

My daughter’s crying intensified. Her mom led her stumbling down the hallway. A deafening silence hung in the air.

Our betrayer, a man I had considered a friend, spoke with accusation. "This is your fault. You should have been nicer to me."

From behind me, Terry declared, "You need to leave—now." His voice was elevated and demanding. "You need to go home to your family and tell your wife what is happening. Wait until one of the bishops calls you. Do you understand it's time for you to go?"

That night, rain came down in sheets and froze solid. You couldn't walk outside without falling down. The cold permeated my body and spirit.

In Psalm 41:9, David said, "Even my close friend, whom I trusted, he who shared my bread, has lifted up his heel against me." This man I had called friend and brother, had betrayed me and my family. I still find it difficult to grasp what he did. I still recall the sick feeling that swept over me as I realized the depth of his betrayal. My heart raced with fear. I was overcome with anxiety as a cascade of images filled my mind. How could this be true?

Our therapist later said that day was V-Day for Heather but D-Day for Annie and me and our entire community. All I could see was devastation—blood, death, hopelessness. I couldn't imagine life beyond this moment.

Within twenty-four hours of Heather's revelation, seven of my fellow bishops and their wives were standing in my kitchen. My dear friends and peers immediately booked flights to Kansas from all over America. Some drove from hours away. The next morning, Annie and I woke up to them making coffee in our kitchen.

They held my wife and daughter. They listened to us express

our fear and anger. They hired professional therapists for Heather and our family. They called the members of our church council to bring them together. They fielded the questions. They took over all of my responsibilities, which included a number of churches. I was instantly on sabbatical.

"You just be Dad," they said. "We will carry everything else."

Five years earlier, I had looked to these men and women to help me sort through my shallow theological quandary, and now they were living out exactly what they professed to believe. If our beliefs cannot be lived out during our greatest battles, then our beliefs are nothing more than unrealized ideals. But here they were—these CEEC bishops and their wives—in my living room, crying with my family, thinking for us when we couldn't. The language they had given me was now made manifest in their behaviors.

These were the good Samaritans who refused to walk by a wounded man lying on the side of the road. Many of our lifelong friends passed us by, though I'm sure they were praying for us. Prayer, however, is more than an act of piety or worship, more than bowing a head or bending a knee, more than offering words to God for those in need. Prayer is an attitude of the soul and an openness toward our friends, our Friend, and our Father. Prayer is living in communion with the Holy Spirit.

The Communion had been modeling convergence to our church for the previous five years. They helped me cultivate an atmosphere of covenantal love. They helped us grow beyond the individualistic, consumer-based, church-growth trap. We were a better people for it. I felt so grateful, not only for the Communion but for the church they had helped us become.

Betrayal is profoundly paralyzing and extremely isolating.

There are moments you can't feel anything and then moments where you feel everything. There is nowhere stable; everything is shaky. It would be months before I could eat or sleep well. We were deeply confused emotionally and spiritually. Not only was my family and church shaken, but my faith was shaken. I was filled with uncertainty. What was true? Was any of the last fifteen years of ministry real or true? Could I trust anyone? Could I trust God? If trust is gone, nothing seems possible.

Years of lies, and secrets! What was wrong with me? What kind of father was I? Was it my fault? What could I have done differently? I think every parent asks themselves these kinds of questions. Abuse is like an atom bomb—its fallout can never be calculated, and its effects are felt for decades.

These deep friendships saved my life and my family. They saved our fellowship. We would have become old and bitter. We would have remained angry with God, with the perpetrator. We would never have made it through this crisis without the true church—a community of covenanted people living in relationship with each other. People who are one with each other. People who care more for others than for themselves. People who know how to suffer with you and never leave. These friends suffered alongside us for the weeks and months that followed. Though I had been betrayed by a beloved friend, I was also being restored by beloved friends.

Jesus sat in the upper room and broke bread with his closest friends—what a moment that must have been. We all want to experience that kind of intimacy. And yet, in the midst of this shared meal, Jesus said, "Assuredly, I say to you, one of you will betray me." Betrayal is only possible when we deeply love and trust, but we cannot let betrayal separate us from relating to others.

Among the many fruits of betrayal that I had to overcome was bitterness and cynicism toward not just my friend but of every man. As Voltaire said, "May God defend me from my friends; I can defend myself from my enemies." Because of this one friend's unfaithfulness, I was faced with a choice: do I now distrust all people? Betrayal often leads to a distrust of everyone and everything, even God. Over the years of pastoring, I have noticed that many women who are cynical about men are actually angry about the unfaithfulness of one man in particular. Anyone who has experienced the shock of an uplifted heel knows this temptation to distrust everyone. But we cannot allow bitterness or cynicism to abide in our souls—it will sneak up like a terrorist and stab from behind.

Betrayal can rob us of our faith in God's goodness, leaving a toxic suspicion that can pollute every other relationship, and in some cases, the entire community. When the virtues of friendship are broken, the virtues of the community are deeply shaken. Though we may experience deep wounds from within our community of faith, we cannot afford to leave the community. Only within this place of union with Christ can we overcome the very wounds that were meant to destroy. I have been this transparent for one reason and one reason only: too many have run too far from home.

I love the church. I'm convinced that Jesus is building his church and that hell cannot defeat her. I believe we must recover the true nature of the church. We must stop the division that keeps us from fulfilling the mission of Christ. We must repent of the deconstruction and apathy for union so that real unity can be realized in our generation. The church must again become that safe, sacred space, the hiding place into which we can run and be made whole.

I know that these statements stir up all kinds of reactions. The church has been divided for so long that we have almost lost all hope that she could be anything other than what we've known. I've been accused of being both naively innocent and ignorant when it comes to the hope I have for the church.

Someone close to me once suggested, "Maybe you're just lucky." She didn't mean it as a compliment. When I asked her to clarify her meaning, she responded, "Yeah, maybe you just haven't experienced the pain in the church. Maybe you've just been lucky."

Without knowing each other's personal histories, we tend to assume things about each other, which is why I decided to share this piece of my journey.

As I ponder how my family survived and indeed thrived through what would have destroyed many, I am convinced that the atmosphere of the church is key. The leadership of my Communion, of my local church, of our family, and our friends were completely united. They were "one"—one with Christ and with each other. Unity creates a sacred space where God's blessing and eternal life is manifested. If unity reveals or makes known God's presence, then disunity hinders such manifestation.

Every time the wind blows, I'm aware that I'm not in control of anything. I don't know where the wind comes from or where it goes. Today, that same room in which the bombs dropped on D-Day is filled little voices—my daughter's children wrestle with Pops, and laughter has replaced the grief. The peace soothes my soul. From the ashes of abuse has arisen life, even abundant life.

I thought I was so strong. I thought I had it all together, but that's the lie. To think, *I've got this. I'll do this thing on my own. I don't need anyone.* The truth is that we all need each other. Whether we acknowledge it or not, we cannot live on our own. That whole "just me and Jesus" attitude—Jesus is a friend who will send you a friend. He said he would never leave you alone. Look around. I promise he is closer than you think.

CHAPTER 13

Father Francis

> "A torn and divided Christianity is, nevertheless, a scandal for which all Christians need deeply to repent."
>
> —David Watson

Sometimes winter seems interminable—the cold simply won't go away. No amount of clothing keeps you warm outside, and there's never enough wood on the fire. Nature plays you for a fool with a day or two of sunshine and short sleeves, but then the wind blows from the north to remind you it's not quite over. The season of healing was truly the winter of my soul.

Archbishop of Canterbury Rowan Williams has talked about living in the church as "profoundly hard work." The next few years were extremely hard work! I had entered a doctoral program at George Fox University in Newburg, Oregon, a few years earlier, which exposed me to friends and ideas that helped secure my spiritual foundation. One such influence was Leonard Sweet, a prolific author and a visiting distinguished professor at George Fox while I was pursuing my doctorate. In his book *Out of the Question, Into the Mystery*, published in 2004, Len argued that we have become relationally deficient—our culture is hungry for authentic relationships with God and each other. But these relationships require that we step beyond our reasoning and logic to embrace the mystery of God's love. Even in the mist of betrayals and relational failures, God reveals his unfailing love. The counterfeit reveals the authentic.

Expressing, experiencing, and sharing the authentic love of God has been at the heart of my personal ministry and that of the CEEC. While my family and community rebuilt itself in the wake of my associate's betrayal, my colleagues in the CEEC continued their great work.

In 2006, during a Catholic Fraternity gathering in Argentina, my friend Tony Palmer met the archbishop of Buenos Aires—a Jesuit cardinal named Jorge Mario Bergoglio. Father Mario had embraced the Catholic Church's charismatic renewal and supported an ecumenical gathering of six thousand Catholics and evangelicals that year in Luna Park, a stadium in downtown Buenos Aires.

Over the next few years, Tony and Father Mario developed a close friendship, one that Pope Francis likened unto father and son. They began to dream about how to bridge the divide between Christians, particularly Roman Catholics and Protestants. I remember Tony's passion to see this dream manifested in our Communion. He and I shared many conversations about this dream of unity in diversity and unity with a purpose. We dreamed of unity that was more than merely being together but one that would facilitate the mission of the church to reach the world with the gospel of Jesus.

During a particular gathering of CEEC bishops, Bishop Tony described some of his conversations with Cardinal Bergoglio about how the work of ecumenism would lead to the evangelization of all people, which ultimately was Jesus's prayer: "I do not pray for these alone, but also for those who will believe in Me through their word; that they all may be one, as You, Father, are in Me, and I in You; that they also may be one in Us, that the world may believe that You sent Me. And the glory which You gave Me I have given them, that they may be one just as We are one: I in them, and You in Me; that they may be made perfect in one, and that the world may know that You have sent Me, and have loved them as You have loved Me." (John 17:20-23)

After another meeting of the bishops that I couldn't attend because of our family situation, Tony called to pray with me. He filled me in on the meeting.

"Quintin, we are part of something so much bigger than we could ever imagine," he said. "Keep dreaming, and remember that all things work together for the good of those who love the Lord and are called according to his purpose. The dream of unity cannot be lost in the midst of our life circumstances."

In October of 2008—two months before I found out about Heather's abuse—at our general synod, the bishops had asked me to serve as ecumenical bishop. Tony reminded me that I still had a role to play in this dream of unity. His passion drew me in—he was good at that. He was a friend who wouldn't allow another friend to stay stuck.

I realized that we can't allow our regrets about the past nor our frustrations over the future to keep us stuck in the moment.

Friends call you down out of trees. Friends stoop into your dust. Friends meet you at a well. They invite you back into the streams of living water or, at the very least, encourage you to remain planted by those streams.

In October of 2011, I attended the annual synod of the National House of Bishops at Redeemer Church in Ponte Vedra Beach, Florida. Every year, the bishops of every diocese in the US come together for fellowship and celebration and to strategize in mission together. Each bishop gives a personal report to the House.

Toward the end of our afternoon session, as I was finishing my report, one of the other bishops interrupted me.

"I think we have found our next presiding bishop," he announced.

I waited, thinking he was going to point out who that might be. I've always been a bit slow on the uptake. *Wait a minute—he's looking in my direction.* I honestly thought he was having fun at my expense. Within a few months, I was installed as the presiding bishop of the Communion that had literally saved my life.

As the presiding bishop over the National House of Bishops, I represent a number of dioceses in the US. I am the presiding bishop of a province, which is a collection of dioceses and orders. I am a bishop of the diocese, which is a collection of churches and ministries. And I am the pastor of a church that includes a multifaceted staff and faithfully baptized congregants.

The national presiding bishop is the ceremonial lead of the CEEC—it's not an authoritative role, and the bishops are averse to any connotations of elitism or hierarchy. We also prefer not to use the term archbishop, which is more of a Catholic, Anglican, or Episcopal title. As presiding bishop, I convene the House of Bishops, but authority rests in the consensus of the House. I call us to gather together with Christ and listen for the Holy Spirit's leading. We speak to, with, for, and from each other. When I speak outside the House, I speak for all of our opinions, not just my own. Throughout our history, there have been people who wanted to centralize authority into a hierarchy, but we have always insisted we're not a hierarchy. Our highest value is relationship because relationship is the only pathway to unity in the body of Christ.

In the spring of 2012, several other bishops and I joined Bishop Tony at the international gathering of the Catholic Fraternity in Assisi, Italy. I wasn't prepared for what a glorious experience I would have in Assisi. The small town was built high on the hillside for protection, with a sweeping view of the valley. Assisi is best known as the birthplace of Saint Francis, a charismatic reformer known for his humility, simplicity, and loving heart. He also founded the Franciscan religious order in 1208. I had been a huge fan of Saint Francis—his calling and teachings had inspired the renaming of our diocese. Surrounded by his story, something strange took place in my soul— a healing, a restoration.

I had brought several books about Saint Francis—I couldn't read enough about him. In his book *The Life of Saint Francis of Assisi*, Bonanventure wrote, "There as he knelt in prayer before a painted image of the Crucified, he felt greatly comforted in spirit and his eyes were full of tears as he gazed at the cross. Then, all of a sudden, he heard a voice come from the cross and telling him three times, 'Francis, go and repair my house. You see it is falling down." Little did I know the story would get even richer.

Raniero Cantalamessa, preacher to the papal household since 1980, preached twice that week. Pope John Paul II first appointed him to the position, and he has continued serving in this capacity under both Pope Benedict XVI and Pope Francis. For the past twelve years, Cantalamessa has been a member of the Catholic Delegation for the dialogue with the Pentecostal churches.

This man mesmerized me. His first sermon was titled "You must be born again." His second sermon was titled, "Have you received the Holy Spirit since you believed?" This Roman Catholic priest preached a better salvation message than any evangelical I have ever heard. I have borrowed liberally from his message on Pentecost, as it's the best sermon ever on being filled with the Holy Spirit. I've been honored to meet with Father Cantalamessa several times over the years.

By the time we left Assisi, I was more convinced than ever that we are living in a unique time in history. The Lord is calling us again to recover and restore the unity of the body of Christ, the house of God.

Christians become entrenched in their tribes and fail to realize the family of God is much larger than we have ever imagined. Pentecostals love being Spirit-filled, but they often forget that the work of the Holy Spirit is ecumenical—the work of the Holy Spirit is to make us one. Where the Spirit is, there is unity. Over the last 150 years since the Pentecostal renewal started, we've become too focused on how many gifts we have, whether it's speaking in tongues, or prophesy, or something else that only reinforces a sense of individualism. The convergence movement recognizes that the Holy Spirit's work is to bring us together in relationship to make us one church, reconciled in our diversity.

Our desire for unity extends beyond just reconciling the splintered Protestant denominations but also bringing Protestants and Catholics closer together. How do we tear down these walls? How do we open the doors? We understand that we may never change the institutions, but we could make strides by walking together as brothers and sisters, as friends, as people relating to one another in the love of Christ. My friend Cal Jernigan once said, “Unity begins with the willingness to see the world through someone else’s eyes.” The dream of unity is powered by friends who are willing to look through one another’s eyes.

On February 28, 2013, Pope Benedict XVI resigned unexpectedly—the first pope to do so in six hundred years. Before his reasons were even understood, the College of Cardinals called a conclave to name his successor. By March, 115 cardinals were sequestered in the Sistine Chapel in the Vatican to begin the voting process, led by the Holy Spirit.

On March 13, the day white smoke poured out of the Sistine Chapel chimney, I was leading a meeting at a Roman Catholic monastery in Ferdinand, Indiana. Several of us who had crowded into a small office watched as Jorge Mario Bergoglio walked out onto the balcony of St. Peter’s Basilica, dressed in white robes.

Several of the monks asked, “Bergoglio, who is he?”

“I know that guy!” I said stunned.

A friend of a friend, Father Mario had become Pope Francis.

For the first time in the history of the Roman Catholic Church, the pope took the name of Saint Francis of Assisi. The work of the Lord is so obvious.

Tony told me the story of when Pope Francis called him after his election.

"Tony, it's Pope Francis," said the voice on the other end of the line.

Tony thought one of his friends was playing a joke. "Oh, that's funny," he said and hung up. His cell phone rang again.

"Tony, really, it's Father Mario, don't hang up."

Over the next several months, Tony met with Pope Francis several times. None of us could have ever imagined this would happen. Tony shared with me his excitement over what he and Father Francis were contemplating. They began to talk about how we might work together and expand the ecumenical conversation with other Christians.

On January 14, 2014, during Tony's meeting with Francis at his Vatican residence, Casa Santa Marta, he told the pope how he planned to attend Kenneth Copeland Ministries' annual Ministers Conference the following month. Despite Tony's migration to the CEEC, he and Brother Copeland remained faithfully involved in each other's ministries. He asked Francis if he would like to send a greeting to the three thousand evangelical leaders who would be in attendance.

Francis asked Tony, "Do you have your phone?"

"I always have my phone," Tony replied.

After a pause, Francis said, "Why don't we make a video?"

Tony pulled out his iPhone and recorded a seven-minute video of Pope Francis addressing his evangelical brothers and sisters in his lyrical native Italian.

"Two rules: love God above all, and love the other, because he is your brother and sister," he began. "With these two rules, we can go ahead.

"It gives me joy that you have come together to worship Jesus Christ, the only Lord. And to pray to the Father and to receive the Spirit. This brings me joy because I can see that God is working all over the world.

"There are families who love each other, and families who don't love each other. Families who come together and families who separate themselves. We are kind of, permit me to say, separated because of all of our sins and misunderstandings throughout history. We all share the blame. We have all sinned. There is only one blameless, the Lord. I yearn for this separation to come to an end and give us communion.

"The holy scriptures speak of when Joseph's brothers [who had sold him into slavery] began to starve from hunger, they went to Egypt to buy bread so that they could eat. They had money, but they couldn't eat the money. But there they found something more than food—they found their brother.

"All of us have currency—the currency of our culture, our history. We have cultural and religious riches, and we have diverse traditions. But we have to encounter each other as brothers. We must cry together like Joseph did. These tears will unite us—the tears of love.

"I speak to you as a brother. Let our yearning grow because this will propel us to find each other and to embrace one another. And together to worship Jesus Christ as the only Lord of history.

"Please pray for me because I need your prayers. And let's pray to the Lord that he unites us all. Come on—we are brothers.

Let's give each other a spiritual hug, and let God complete the work that he has begun. . . He will complete this miracle of unity."*

One of the hopes of ecumenism has been to share communion together, breaking bread at a shared table. However, the institutional church - even with a reformer like Francis at the head - is still in opposition to this shared meal. But what Francis asserted is that we are brothers through our shared baptism. Bread is secondary to the brotherhood. We have to learn to be brothers first. Pope Francis's words were a balm on many hearts—to hear from a Catholic pontiff that all Christians are brothers and sisters. This is where true communion is found.

What's a dream for us is a nightmare for those who insist on maintaining the historic splits, doctrinal divisions, judgments, and misunderstandings that have kept us separate for hundreds of years. A division has long existed within the church and our societies. The two evils that prevent Protestants, Catholics, and our various sects and denominations from being friends are institutionalism and individualism. Both of these have kept us divided for centuries. They have robbed generations of saints of their song. Every one of us have been created to hear the sound of the creator singing songs of deliverance over us. Deliverance from the limitations that have been self-imposed or forced on us by others. Deliverance from the consumerism of our generation. Deliverance from the differences that have caused us to fear one another and that have kept us apart for far too long. Our desire to live meaningful lives is not found in the spiritual

---

* Tony Palmer, "The Miracle of Unity Has Begun," February 28, 2014, https://www.youtube.com/watch?v=NHbEWw7l_Ek.

individualism or in stale institutionalism but rather in being friends.

The video of Pope Francis went viral, and Tony found himself bombarded with emails from other evangelicals and charismatics who wanted to be part of the movement toward Christian unity. As Tony stated in his video, "The real gift of communion is finding our brother. For those of us who have ears to hear, let us hear, because this is both profound and revolutionary. Pope Francis is calling us into an authentic communion based on the fact that we are brothers and sisters in Christ, not communion through our common traditions. This is a new way forward."

We were living a dream.

On July 20, 2014, a beautiful Sunday morning, I was excited to preach to our congregation. I was expecting to hear from Tony in a couple of days, as we had much to catch up on. He had met with Pope Francis a few weeks earlier, and I knew that they had discussed our upcoming meeting with Francis later in the year. Tony had then flown to South Africa from Rome to facilitate an intercommunion relationship between another communion and the CEEC before finally returning home to England. Things were happening so fast. The news of our relationship with Pope Francis had initiated all kinds of conversations in the US and around the world.

While I delivered my sermon, I heard my wife gasp out loud. She looked up from the front row with tears filling her eyes. She held out her cell phone to me, and I reached down and took it. I still can't process what I read. That same day, Tony was riding his motorcycle near his home in England when he was struck by a car. One of our mutual friends had texted to see if I knew anything. I finished the service, not remembering anything else

I said besides asking the church to pray.

Ten hours of surgery later, Tony died of his injuries. He was only forty-eight years old. He left behind his wife, Emiliana, and their two children. I can't begin to describe the shock.

On August 5, I flew to Birmingham, England, where Bishop David Carr met me. The next morning, we drove to Bath for Tony's funeral, which was held at Saint John the Evangelist Roman Catholic Church. When we walked into the narthex, the parish priest, Father David Ryan, a truly kind and Spirit-filled believer, greeted us.

Father David explained that he wanted us to join him in leading the procession into the sanctuary and to remain at the front on either side of the altar in the choir stalls. He asked our forgiveness for not being able to allow us to concelebrate the Mass with him, but his diocesan bishop simply wouldn't permit it. Pope Francis, however, had given the directive that Tony be buried as a bishop. Pope Francis had often referred to him as "my bishop brother, Tony Palmer."

"Of course, as the representative of the CEEC, you will address the gathering and give whatever remarks that you would like," said Father David.

I hadn't expected any of this at all. To be included in the service was humbling.

I had several letters to give to Emiliana, including letters from Archbishop Robert Wise and Archbishop Charles Travis. During the service, I read them and then shared my personal condolences to Tony's widow and their children. As I spoke, I was struck by a prophetic vision—this beautiful old building was under repair. Metal scaffolding covered one side of the church from floor to ceiling, stretching from the back of the church all the way to the front where Tony's coffin had been placed. Here lay a man who shared the same dream as Saint Francis of Assisi and Pope Francis, a call "go and repair my house which, as you can see, is in ruins."

Tony's widow, Emiliana, read a moving note from his dear friend, Pope Francis: "We were great friends. Many times, we prayed in the same Spirit. Those of us who love him feel impelled by his zeal to follow in his footsteps, to walk without rest preparing the bride, one single bride for the bridegroom who will come."

CHAPTER 14

Jubilee

"Some of us believe that God is almighty and can do everything; and that he is all wise and may do everything; but that he is all-love and will do everything—there we draw back. As I see it, this ignorance is the greatest of all hindrances to God's lovers."

—Julian of Norwich

In October of 2014, in keeping with Tony's plan, I joined a group of twenty other CEEC bishops from around the world in Rome to meet with Pope Francis privately, only now our agenda including mourning Tony together. Pope Francis had invited us to meet with him to weep together and in hopes that we might continue to work together for the unity of Protestants and Catholics.

Ahead of our first meeting, Julia, a secretary for the Catholic

Charismatic Renewal, guided our bishops through this visit and advised us on what would happen the next day when we met with him. The main reason she wanted to meet with us was to tell us about the person she had known for more than two decades—the man he was before he became Pope Francis. She shared his history and communicated the human side of Pope Francis.

She told us that he was a pastor first and always—he loved people and had a tremendous heart for the poor. She told us that he believes the kingdom of God is first and foremost relational and moves forward because of relationship; therefore, he wanted to spend time getting to know us.

"He hates being called Holy Father or Your Eminence," she said. "He's not a monarch, nor your pope. He's the bishop of Rome. He'd just prefer you call him Father Francis or Francis. Either one."

Sure enough, anytime I've called him, "Your Holiness," Francis has replied, "No, no, no—I'm Father Francis."

Julia explained Father Francis's personal relationship with Christ and his passion to see Christ's church healed of division. Those passions were what had fueled his relationship with Tony.

If there had been any question as to what Father Francis wanted from us, it was quickly answered. During our meeting, he announced that he was grateful that Emiliana and Archbishop Robert Wise had agreed to "carry the torch, this dream, which was Tony's, this dream of being able to walk in communion. Our shared baptism is more important than our differences. We all believe in the Father, the Son and the Holy Spirit."

The heart of every meeting with Father Francis has been

about unity—he has a huge heart for the unity of the body of Christ. Though the Vatican as an institution may never allow Protestants to share the Eucharistic table, charismatic Catholics and the CEEC will continue to pray together that we recognize our shared baptism.

When Tony once considered joining the Roman Catholic Church, Francis was quick to disagree. "Don't join the church," he said. "You are the church. We are brothers by baptism. If we believe in Jesus, then we're brothers. If we love one another, we're brothers."

During our meeting in 2014, Father Francis asked us to trust him and to keep being a bridge. "We need to have bridge builders," he said. "The Catholic Church needs to be more evangelical, and the evangelical church needs to be more Catholic."

We asked Pope Francis how to walk out this journey from day to day. How do we make ecumenicalism practical? The general approach to ecumenism has always been left to the theologians, but Pope Francis had a fresh approach.

"We need theologians—they are important!" he said with a smile. He has thanked theologians for their important and tedious work, but he has also encouraged a more relational approach.

"Do you know a priest?" he asked. "Would you buy him a cup of coffee? Okay, we make a photo together. When you buy a priest a cup of coffee, you show him the photo and tell him we're friends."

Friends, a novel idea. Pope Francis wonderfully conveyed the essence of this relational ecumenism by inviting us to have supper with him in Casa Santa Marta. We had only been seated a few minutes when Pope Francis stood up, took a bottle of wine from the table, and began to serve the bishop next to him. The staff were shocked. We were shocked. The room fell silent as the pontiff of Rome poured wine into several glasses, waving off our protest. After he had filled more than a few glasses, he handed off the bottle to another bishop who then continued around the table.

Relational ecumenism is the way to realize the unity of the church.

After dinner, he took a personal photograph with each of us, a day none of us will ever forget. Since that moment, every one of us has reached out to every Catholic priest or bishop we know to ask if they would be willing to grab a cup of coffee. This relational ecumenism isn't theoretical but lived and experienced. In an environment of friendship, we come to know and discover that we are brothers and sisters in the risen Christ.

Shortly after I returned from Rome, I called a Catholic bishop in my region and asked if he would meet with me. We set a date, and when I got to his office, there on his desk was a framed picture of him with Pope Francis.

I pulled up my photo on my phone. "I have one of those, too."

He sat down in his chair and smiled. "We have to be the only two people in Kansas with a photo with the pope."

Not one person I've invited has ever refused the offer. I now have relationships with Catholic clergy in Kansas, Nebraska, Oklahoma, and Oregon. We dialogue without trying to resolve our differences.

My Pentecostal friends think we've sold out to being Catholic, and the Catholics think that Francis is trying to deconstruct the church. But despite the constant swirl of conspiracy theories, the CEEC, the Catholic Charismatic Renewal, and other groups have continued to move forward in our desire to bring like-minded people together to celebrate the unity of the church. Unity is a pedestrian pilgrimage, lived one step at a time.

In 2016, I was elected presiding bishop of the CEEC's International House of Bishops, which represents jurisdictions from around the world. The international presiding bishop serves as a symbol of unity for the International House of Bishops. Because each of our provinces are self-governing, I don't have to lord over them; instead, I continually call us back to the center of those values that hold us together. I convene and chair the meetings with the International House of Bishops, and we work together to build consensus and keep our focus on the essentials of our faith so that our unity with each other and our witness are held together. As Saint Augustine said, "In essentials, unity; in nonessentials, liberty; in all things, charity." We do this so that the Communion, while providing apostolic structure and connection, can continue to function as an organic and relational movement.

I communicate to the International House of Bishops any urgent needs or requests so that they can be addressed. I also serve as chief ecumenical officer when dealing with the wider church beyond our Communion, and when I do, I speak for the whole, not simply for myself, while staying sensitive to anything that might harm or disrupt our unity.

Our communion has a presence on six continents and in more than twenty countries. I knew that it was (and still is) too early to discern what will come next in this work the Holy Spirit brought about through Tony and Francis. The wound of

Tony's death is still raw, and from the moment Tony took out his iPhone to film Francis, no one has been following a script.

One possibility stemmed from a draft document that Tony presented to Pope Francis in June of 2014, which included three elements. The first was the Nicene Creed, which Catholics and evangelicals share. The second was the core of the Joint Declaration on the Doctrine of Justification, an accord signed in 1999 in Augsburg, Germany, by leaders from the Lutheran World Federation and the Roman Catholic Church, making clear there is no disagreement over justification by faith. And the final section asserted that Catholics and evangelicals are now united in mission because we are declaring the same gospel.

Tony's dream was that Protestant and Catholic leaders would sign the document sometime in 2017, during the 500th anniversary of the Reformation and the fiftieth anniversary of the Catholic charismatic renewal. This document wasn't intended to be an instrument of organizational unity but rather a sign and symbol of our love for one another.

That same year, Pope Francis moved to consolidate the two primary charismatic organizations within the Roman Catholic Church—the Catholic Fraternity and International Catholic Charismatic Renewal Services (ICCRS)—into a unified service called Catholic Charismatic Renewal International Service (CHARIS) to serve the nearly 200 million charismatic Catholics across the world.

The timing on the merger was significant because the following year was the Golden Jubilee to commemorate the fiftieth anniversary of the Catholic Charismatic Renewal—the famous Duquesne weekend, an ecumenical charismatic movement resulting from Pentecostals praying over Catholics to receive the Holy Spirit. Prior to his death, Tony had been working with Francis in preparation for the Jubilee, but after his death, I found myself unexpectedly communicating with Francis' office on this initiative and others, which was meant to foster unity between Catholics and Protestants.

My meeting with Francis just after Easter in 2017 centered on the Golden Jubilee—a celebration of this outpouring of the Holy Spirit on the Catholic Church and the ecumenism that followed. Like those of us in the CEEC, Francis believes that the work of the Holy Spirit is to create unity. That was the day he said to me, "The music is the same."

On Saturday, June 3, 2017, the Golden Jubilee took place at Circus Maximus, the site of the ancient chariot-racing stadium and Christian martyrdom prior to Constantine. More than 50,000 worshippers from 121 different countries gathered before a massive stage that held seventy-five people. Seated on stage were seven CEEC bishops, Robert Wise, Sean Yost, David Carr, Ed Gungor, Ryan Mackey, and myself, as well as our guests, Glenn Burris Jr., president of the Foursquare Church; Sammy Rodriguez, lead pastor of New Season and president of the National Hispanic Christian Leadership Conference; Chris Seay, lead pastor of Ecclesia Houston and president of Ecclesia Bible Society; author Sarah Bessey; Father Michael Sparough; David Wells, general superintendent of the Pentecostal Assemblies of Canada; and Billy Wilson, president of Oral Roberts University.

Pope Francis addressed the crowd beneath a clear blue sky. He began by recounting the story in the Acts of the Apostles when Jesus ordered the disciples not to leave Jerusalem but to wait for the promise of the Father—John baptized with water, but they would be baptized with the Holy Spirit.

On the day of Pentecost, everyone heard the sound of a mighty rushing wind fill the house, and what appeared to be tongues of fire rested upon them. The power of the Holy Spirit came upon everyone, and worshippers from many nations, tribes, and tongues became the first members of the church. They didn't speak the same language, nor did they possess an agreed-upon doctrine. But they were all possessed by the Holy Spirit and joined together as one. They began sharing life together. This new community of people were called the ecclesia, which means "a called-out assembly," or more commonly in Hebrew, "a gathering together." This ecclesia was and still is the work of the Holy Spirit. The church was and is a relational community because God is a relational God.

"Today, we are here in a kind of upper room beneath the open sky, unafraid," said Francis, "with our hearts open to the promise of the Father. 'All of us who believe' have gathered here, all who confess that Jesus is Lord. The Holy Spirit has brought us together to build bonds of fraternal friendship that encourage us on our journey toward unity for mission—not to stand still but to proclaim that Jesus is Lord, *Jesús es el Señor*. To proclaim together the love of the Father for all his children. To proclaim the Good News to all peoples. To demonstrate that peace is possible if we are at peace with one another.

"If we emphasize our differences, we are at war among ourselves, and we cannot proclaim peace. We have differences, but we desire to be a reconciled diversity. We should not forget that phrase but say it to everyone: reconciled diversity. The phrase is not mine; it comes from a Lutheran brother, reconciled diversity.

"We are here, and we are many! We have gathered to pray together to ask the Holy Spirit to come upon each of us so that we can go forth into the streets of the city and the world to proclaim the lordship of Jesus Christ. . . . There are differences, but the Spirit enables us to understand the message of Jesus's resurrection, each in his or her our own language.

"We are gathered here to celebrate the sovereign work of the Holy Spirit in the church that occurred fifty years ago and gave rise to—an institution? No. An organization? No. A flood of grace—the flood of grace of the Catholic Charismatic Renewal. A work that was born—Catholic? No. It was born ecumenical! It was born ecumenical because it is the Holy Spirit who creates unity and the same Spirit who granted the inspiration for this!

"The coming of the Holy Spirit transforms fearful men into courageous witnesses of Jesus. Peter, who had denied Jesus three times, filled with the power of the Holy Spirit proclaims: 'Let all the house of Israel know assuredly that God has made him both Lord and Christ, this Jesus whom you crucified" (Acts 2:36). This is the profession of faith of every Christian. It is ours, all of us, the same!

"Today, we have chosen to gather here in this place where Christians were martyred for the entertainment of onlookers. Today, there are more martyrs than then! Those who kill Christians do not ask, 'Are you Orthodox? Are you Catholic? Are you Evangelical? Are you Lutheran? Are you Calvinist?' No. They ask, 'Are you Christian?' And when they say yes, they immediately slit their throats. This is the ecumenism of blood. The witness of our martyrs brings us together today."

Father Francis had repeatedly encouraged us all to understand the importance of this ecumenism of blood. If our enemies believe we are all one, maybe it's time we believe it, too.

"Christian unity is more urgent than ever," he continued.

"Christians united by the power of the Holy Spirit in prayer and in action on behalf of the most vulnerable. To walk together, to work together, and to love each other. And together, to seek to explain our differences, to come to agreement, but as we keep walking. If we stop walking, we will never come to agreement. This is how it is, because the Holy Spirit wants us to be on the move.

"Fifty years of the Catholic Charismatic Renewal. A flood of grace of the Spirit! And why a flood of grace? Because it has no founder, no bylaws, no structure of governance. Clearly, it has given rise to many expressions that are surely works inspired by the Spirit, with various charisms, and all in the service of the church. . . .

"The most precious gift that all of us have received is baptism. And now the Spirit is leading us on this journey of conversion sweeping across the entire Christian world, which is another reason why the Catholic Charismatic Renewal is a special place for pursuing the path to unity.

"This flood of grace is for the whole church, not just for some. None of us is master—we are all servants of this flood of grace. Along with this experience, you constantly remind the church of the power of prayer and praise. Praise that is the prayer of gratitude and thanksgiving for God's gracious love. . . . Jubilation, cheer, joy, that is the fruit of the Holy Spirit! Either a Christian experiences joy in his or her heart, or something is wrong. The joy of proclaiming the good news of the Gospel!"

Francis concluded his address by reminding us that charismatic renewal also must play out in service to humanity and helping those in need.

"Baptism in the Holy Spirit, praise, and social action—these three things are inseparably linked," he said. "To share baptism in the Holy Spirit with everyone in the Church, to praise the Lord unceasingly, to walk together with Christians of different churches and ecclesial communities in prayer and activity on behalf of those in greatest need, to serve the poor and the sick. This is what the church and the pope expect from you, Catholic Charismatic Renewal, but also from everyone here: all of you who have become part of this flood of grace."*

Bishop Tony Palmer used to say, "Division is diabolical, but diversity is divine." I thought of our late friend when Francis shared the concept of "reconciled diversity." Unity is the gift the church has received, not something she has achieved. The identity of this community transcends all other distinctions. Diversity, not uniformity, is celebrated as one of its core values—unity in the midst of diversity. The people of God come from "every tribe and tongue." The image of people reconciled with one another in the midst of such diversity is a beautiful picture of the church. In a world polarized by politics, divided by denominations, traumatized by tribes, and castrated by culture, the church needs to recover its authentic nature of "unity in diversity."

The body of Christ reveals that the church is more than an organization of people around a common cause—rather, it's a living organism, the continuation of Christ's presence in the world. The body of Christ is united to him in his death and resurrection and now lives out of that union. The basis of our faith is our friendship that is a gift from God.

Ignatius of Antioch (50-108 AD) described the church "as a

---

* Jackie Morgan, "Address of His Holiness Pope Francis at the Golden Jubilee," Western Oregon Catholic Charismatic Renewal, June 29, 2017, https://woccr.org/address-holiness-pope-francis-golden-jubilee/

choir able to sing in unison and with one voice."* Or, as Father Francis said during our meeting after Easter in 2017, "The music is the same." We are a communion, not a denomination. We are a movement, not an institution. We are a living breathing organism, not an organization. We are friends!

⁂

Two years later, on July 8, 2019, I sat before Pope Francis once again while he addressed ten thousand people gathered at the CHARIS international conference.

In remarking on the merger between the Catholic Fraternity and the ICCRS, he said, "Today, one thing ends, and another begins. A new stage of this journey marked by communion between all members of the charismatic family, in which the mighty presence of the Holy Spirit has manifested for the good of the entire church. . . .

"You asked me to tell you what the pope and the church expect from this new service—from CHARIS and the entire Charismatic Renewal. I expect to share baptism in the Holy Spirit with everyone in the church. It is the grace you have received. Share it! Don't keep it to yourselves!

"I expect to serve the unity of the body of Christ, the church, the community of believers in Jesus Christ. This is very important, for the Holy Spirit creates unity but also diversity. The personality of the Holy Spirit is interesting: with the charisms he creates the greatest diversity, but then he harmonizes the charisms in unity. Saint Basil says that 'the Holy Spirit is harmony'—he

---

* Robert E. Webber, *Ancient-Future Faith: Rethinking Evangelicalism for a Postmodern World* (Grand Rapids: Baker, 1999), 80.

creates harmony in the Spirit and harmony among us.

"And to serve the poor and those in greatest need, physical or spiritual. This does not mean, as some might think, that suddenly the Renewal has become communist. No, it has become evangelical, for this is in the Gospel.

"These three things—baptism in the Holy Spirit, unity in the body of Christ, and service to the poor—are the forms of witness that, by virtue of baptism, all of us are called to give for the evangelization of the world. Not proselytism but first and foremost a witness of love. That was what impressed those who encountered the first Christians: 'See how they love one another.'

"Sometimes, of not a few communities it can be said: 'See how they gossip about one another!' This does not come from the Holy Spirit. To evangelize is to share God's love for every man, woman, and child. Offices for evangelization can be established, programs can be carefully planned and implemented, but without love, without community, they are useless!"

See how they love one another.

Francis is eighty-two—I pray that his successor continues his legacy rather than swing the pendulum back the opposite direction. Protestants need to recognize that Catholics are Christians. My dear friend from high school, Pat, was the first to open my eyes to this truth, and another Roman Catholic led me into the real presence of the Holy Spirit.

Protestantism isn't the opposite of Catholicism. Evangelicals aren't the opposite of Catholics. Fundamentalism, however, is the opposite of both. As Francis said, "Fundamentalists believe they're the only ones in the Father's house, but we believe there are many rooms in the Father's house."

During the CHARIS gathering, I had the honor of greeting the delegates. I was overwhelmed by the reality that the only reason I was there was because of a friend with whom I shared a dream that more and more of us are dreaming.

"I am the presiding bishop of the CEEC," I said, "but honestly, I am simply a friend of a friend, and that is why I am here."

The day after Tony's funeral back in August of 2014, I had written the following words in my journal:

I simply am a friend of a friend.
Everything I've ever done,
Everywhere I've ever gone,
Everything that I am;
    all of my life is the result of friendship.
I met my wife because of a friend.
I discovered my own personality because of a friend.
I do what I do because of a friend.
I have become who I am because of a friend.
I have gone around the world,
    all because of the friends in my life.

I simply am who I am because of friends in my life!

After the meeting, a friend said, "There's only one Quintin Moore. Just be yourself. Just be you. There's only one CEEC. Just be who God's called you to be. I want you to know I'm committed to you."

Just be you.

For weeks, those words resonated in my life because everything I have done in the last five years has been to honor Tony's legacy and serve Francis the best way I know how, by living out our calling for relational ecumenism. I have cherished my relationship with Father Francis. Throughout my life, the way I have experienced and expressed the character of God has been in the receiving and sharing of friendship. My journey has been one of friendship that continued to lead me deeper into the Christian faith—a faith that has led me into the dream of the unity.

Jesus told his followers, "Go make disciples." Perhaps we could rephrase that as, "Go make friends."

A writer named François Aussermain once wrote, "Nothing is ever lost; things only become irretrievable. What is lost, then, it is the method of their retrieval and what we discover is not the thing itself, but the overgrown path, the secret staircase, the ancient sewer."*

We forget, or we stop passing the way on to the next generation. We devalue the traditions for something new and exciting. The paths, the staircases, the ancient ways are lost until somehow you stumble forward and suddenly you know you are close.

When you enter Casa Santa Marta, where Pope Francis lives, you descend twenty or so steps into an underground structure similar to a basement, almost half in the ground and half aboveground. After my first visit to Rome, it dawned on me that I had just had my third basement education. From the Nazarene basement in Severy to the basement at Christ Lutheran to this sacred place, the basement of the pope's current residence.

---

* Leonard Sweet, *So Beautiful: Divine Design for Life and the Church* (Colorado Springs: David C. Cook, 2009), 13.

Each time, a friend was opening up the Christian faith to me. Each time, I had to walk down the steps—I had to go lower in order to go higher.

Authentic Christian faith has never been lost. The ancient sewer has been hidden from sight by the abuse and counterfeit offerings of religion, politics, and culture. Relationship remains the "method of retrieval." My life has been marked by both generous friendships and costly friendships. But the truth remains: it is only through friendship that we access our union with God and each other.

A couple of weeks after I returned from Rome, one of my friends, a fellow bishop in the CEEC, called and asked if I would come to Nashville to accompany him to a doctor's appointment that Thursday. I stepped off of Flight 2134 from Wichita to Atlanta, grateful they had changed the arrival gate from A24 to B31. My connection to Nashville was B32, right across the way. Originally, I only had thirty-three minutes to make my connection, and we were twenty minutes late leaving Wichita, leaving only a ten-minute window. I was grateful to walk right off the plane and across the walkway to the next gate just as they were calling my section to board.

As I stepped into the line, two boisterous ladies followed me, engrossed in conversation. I often remind my grandchildren to use their "inside voice," and I had to control the same impulse as we edged toward the ticket counter. They were obviously excited about getting to Nashville—they had traveled from Virginia to attend the PBS Annual Meeting and were discussing in great detail all they had planned for the next few days.

Once on the plane, one of the women sat beside me and the other in front of us. They talked me up the entire flight—discussing their Ivy League alma maters, their husbands' businesses, the boards on which they served, and various other details about their high-flying lifestyles.

Just as the plane was descending into the Nashville airport, one of them finally asked me, "So, what do you do?"

My first thought was, *There's nothing left for me to do—you've done it all!*

But I simply said, "I'm just a friend. I've spent my life just being a friend."

About the Author

Quintin Moore is the senior pastor of The Father's House, a Convergent congregation in Hutchinson, Kansas, and a spiritual leader in the community.

He is currently the presiding bishop of the Communion of Evangelical Episcopal Churches (CEEC), a family of Christian churches and worship communities around the world formed largely as a result of the convergent movement. He founded the Diocese of Restoration in 2004, a network of regional churches. Quintin also founded Sowers of Love, a missionary nonprofit through which he has accompanied people all over the world to spread the gospel of unconditional love. He has assisted in the successful planting of hundreds of churches in the US, Mexico, and other countries around the world, most of which are still thriving in their various communities.

His work advocating for unity in the church has brought him into a circle of friendship with the highest-ranking priests in the Catholic community, where together they educate other believers from different denominations that there is only one true church.

He holds a Bachelor of Science in Leadership and a Master of Ministry from Southwestern Christian University in Bethany, Oklahoma.

Quintin considers his family his greatest wealth and grandest achievement. Married in 1977, he and his wife, Annie, have been inseparable since high school. They have four grown children and 10 grandkids — and counting! Over the course of their marriage, they have fostered seventeen other children.

In his downtime, Quintin can be found at Table Rock Lake, either on his porch or enjoying the open air on his boat.

"Remember no man is a failure who has friends."
— It's a Wonderful Life, 1946

CPSIA information can be obtained
at www.ICGtesting.com
Printed in the USA
BVHW071912060320
573910BV00002B/8